THE SLIM LIVING COOKBOOK

The Slim Living Cookbook
Jo Ann Ploeger

Tyndale House Publishers, Inc., Wheaton, Illinois

DEDICATION

With fond affection to the American and Canadian YMCA staffers who have enthusiastically endorsed the concept of Slim Living and shared it with others.

With appreciation to Sue Mosher, Sue Wefel, Jean De Lacy, and Beth Rutkofske for typing and carrying the burden of bringing this book to completion.

With thanks to readers from around the country for sharing their favorite recipes.

And most of all, with love to Jack, who supports and understands, and to Jill and Laura Lee, whom I pray grow up slim and healthy.

Scripture references are from The Living Bible (TLB) Copyright © 1971 by Tyndale House Publishers and from the King James Version of the Bible, unless otherwise noted.

Second printing, August 1982

Library of Congress Catalog Card Number 81-50847
ISBN 0-8423-5911-7
Copyright © 1981 by Jo Ann Ploeger
Printed in the United States of America

CONTENTS

Renew... Refresh... Be aware....
Our bodies and our spirits need to be renewed every
day. That's why our habits, especially eating habits,
are so important. It is my hope that the over 500
recipes in this book will help you realize the refreshing quality of wholesome food. This awareness
will have the added benefit of helping you manage
weight control. Remember the words from 1 Corinthians 6:19:

*Don't you know that your body is the temple of the Holy
Spirit, who lives in you, and was given to you by God?
You do not belong to yourselves but to God; he bought
you for a price. So use your bodies for God's glory.*

(TEV)

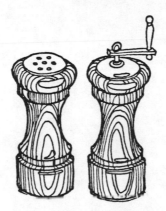

MAKING THE MOST OF THIS BOOK

Maintaining a healthful eating pattern is a worthwhile goal, but good eating habits don't happen overnight. They're the pursuit of a lifetime, especially if you want to live slim! So think, plan, create, and enjoy.

Reminders:
You are free to indulge in vegetables from Group A.

Favor fruits for their fiber, vitamins, and minerals, but don't overdo them.

When possible, use fresh fruit; otherwise, use frozen or canned fruit in its own juice or in another natural fruit juice.

Watch the bread and cereal intake. High fiber content in your breads is important.

Eat meats as if they were ten dollars a pound. We need less than we imagine.

Try to avoid sugar of all kinds: white and brown sugars, honey, and molasses. We suggest artificial sweeteners.

Go easy on fats. Mayonnaise, oil, nuts, bacon, and salad dressing are high in calories. Make a little go a long way.

Drink 4-6 glasses of water everyday. It helps clean out impurities.

Be aware of the protein, fruit, and milk amounts in the recipes. Otherwise, you'll be consuming extra calories without realizing it!

The following suggestions are taken from the YMCA Slim Living Weight Management Program. Study the suggested choices and amounts. Plan your menus in advance—a day ahead, if not a full week.

SUGGESTED DAILY OUTLINE OF BASIC FOODS
FOR A SLIM LIFE

BREAKFAST

High vitamin C fruit (see list)
Protein food—choose ONE:
  1 oz. Swiss or Muenster cheese
  1 egg
  1 oz. cooked or canned fish
  2 oz. cottage cheese, farmer, pot, or ricotta
Bread or cereal, whole grain *or* enriched—choose ONE:
  1 slice bread
  1/2 cup cooked cereal
  3/4 cup ready to eat cereal
Coffee or tea, if desired

LUNCH

Protein Food—Choose ONE:
  2 oz. fish, poultry, *or* lean meat
  2 oz. Swiss or Muenster cheese
  2 oz. cottage cheese
  1 Tbsp. peanut butter
Bread, whole grain or enriched . . . 1 slice
Vegetables—Group A: 3 to 5 choices, raw *or* cooked—(see list)
Beverage, if desired

DINNER

Protein Food—Choose One:
  3-4 oz. cooked fish, poultry, or lean meat
Vegetables—Group A: 2 or more servings
          Group B: 1/2 cup cooked or raw
Beverage, if desired

OTHER DAILY FOODS

Fats: choose 3 from list
Milk: 2 cups skimmed *or* buttermilk *or* 2/3 cup skimmed evaporated
Fruit: 3 servings from list

FOOD FACTS AND CHOICES

Limit lean beef, pork, and lamb to 12 oz. total per week
Limit eggs to 4 per week
Limit hard cheeses to 4 oz. per week
Good low-fat meat choices are fish, chicken without skin, veal, and turkey

Note:

Men could add 2 extra bread choices per day and an extra fruit amount.

FRUIT CHOICES: Choose 3 daily with no sugar added

Apple, 1 small (2" diam.)	Banana, 1/2 small
Applesauce, 1/2 cup	Berries (blackberries, raspberries,
Apricots, fresh, 2 medium	*strawberries), 1 cup
Apricots, dried, 4 halves	*Orange, 1 small
Blueberries, 2/3 cup	*Orange juice, 1/2 cup
*Cantaloupe, 1/4 (6" diam.)	Papaya, 1/3 medium
Cherries, 10 large	Peach, 1 medium
Dates, 2	Pear, 1 small
Figs, fresh, 1 large	Pineapple, 1/2 cup
Figs, dried, 1 large	Pineapple juice, 1/3 cup
*Grapefruit, 1/2 small	Plums, 2 medium
*Grapefruit juice, 1/2 cup	Prunes, 2 dried

Grapes, 12
Grape juice, 1/4 cup
Honeydew melon, 1/8 (7" diam.)
Mango, 1/2 small

Raisins, 2 Tbsp.
*Tangerine, 1 large
Watermelon, 1 cup

*These fruits are rich sources of vitamin C; one serving a day should be used.

Note:
If using canned fruits, get them in their own juice.

VEGETABLES:

Group A—You may eat any amount of these vegetables, if they are uncooked. If cooked, a single cupful at 25 calories is permitted.

Asparagus	Beet greens	Okra
*Broccoli	Chard	*Parsley
*Brussels sprouts	Collards	*Peppers, green or red
Cabbage	Dandelion	Radishes
Cauliflower	Kale	Romaine
Celery	Mustard	Rhubarb (without sugar)
*Chicory	Poke	Sauerkraut
Cucumber	Spinach	String beans, young
Eggplant	Turnips, greens	Summer squash
*Escarole	Lettuce	*Tomatoes
*Greens	Mushrooms	*Watercress

Group B—One serving equals 1/2 cup *or* 40 calories

Beets	Onions	Pumpkin	*Squash, winter
*Carrots	Peas, green	Rutabagas	Turnips

*These vegetables have a high vitamin A content; at least one serving a day should be used.

FATS: Choose three daily

1 tsp. vegetable oil
1 tsp. mayonnaise
2 tsp. French dressing
1 tsp. margarine (with liquid vegetable oil listed first on label of ingredients)
1 slice bacon (be careful with weekly amounts)
6 small nuts

FOODS THAT NEED NOT BE MEASURED:

Coffee
Tea
Clear broth
Bouillon (fat free)
Lemon juice
Gelatin (unsweetened)
Rennet tablets

Mustard
Sweeteners
Pepper, spices
Seasonings
Vinegar
Sugar-free soft drinks
Club soda

Measure Equivalents:
2 oz. = 1/4 cup
8 oz. = 1 cup

To help you get a feel for planning your menus and for working with food exchange totals, we've included a suggested daily outline of basic foods, as well as sample recipes with their food exchange equivalents. Study the following charts, and in a short time you'll be able to gauge the number of portions and equivalents found in any recipe!

BERRY PANCAKES (page 64)

Ingredients	*Food Exchange Equivalents*
1 slice white bread	1 bread
1 egg	1 protein
6-8 drops sweetener, *optional*	no calories
1/2 cup fresh *or* frozen berries	1 fruit
Food Exchange Total:	1 bread
	1 protein
	1 fruit

ORIENTAL CHICKEN (page 105)

Ingredients	*Food Exchange Equivalents*
1 chicken, skinned and halved	4 4-oz. portions
1 cup orange juice	2 fruits
8 drops sweetener	minimal caloric value
1 Tbsp. soy sauce	minimal caloric value
1 tsp. onion powder	minimal caloric value
1 tsp. dried parsley	minimal caloric value
1/2 cup pineapple juice	1 fruit
1 tsp. ginger	minimal caloric value
1/2 cup celery chopped	Group A vegetable
1/2 cup chopped green pepper	Group A vegetable
1 cup mushrooms	Group A vegetable
1 can bean sprouts, drained	Group A vegetable
orange slices (garnish)	minimal caloric value
Food Exchange Total:	4 meats
	3 fruits

Reminder: Group A vegetables may be eaten raw in any amounts. If cooked, 1 cup is permitted.

SPRING VEGETABLE MEDLEY (page 83)

Ingredients	*Food Exchange Equivalents*
1 10-oz. pkg. frozen peas	Group B vegetable
1 8-oz. can water chestnuts, sliced	Group B vegetable
2 Tbsp. powdered chicken bouillon	minimal caloric value
1 Tbsp. cornstarch	minimal caloric value
1/2 tsp. seasoned salt	minimal caloric value
1/4 tsp. garlic powder	minimal caloric value
1/2 cup water	no calories
2 tsp. margarine	1 fat
1 cup halved cherry tomatoes	Group A vegetable

Food Exchange Total: 1 fat

Reminder: Group A vegetables may be eaten raw in any amounts; Group B vegetables amount to 40 calories per 1/2 cup. This entire recipe totals about 75 calories, so enjoy it!

CREAM OF CELERY SOUP (page 30)

Ingredients	*Food Exchange Equivalents*
1 small minced onion	Group A vegetable
3 cups finely chopped celery	Group A vegetable
3 1/2 cups chicken broth	minimal caloric value
2 Tbsp. flour	minimal caloric value
3 Tbsp. water	no calories
1 1/2 cups evaporated skim milk	3 milks
salt and pepper to taste	no calories

Food Exchange Total: 3 milks

PINEAPPLE CRISP (page 131)

Ingredients	*Food Exchange Equivalents*
1/2 cup pineapple chunks	1 fruit
1/3 cup instant milk powder	1 milk
1/4 cup water	no calories

Food Exchange Total: 1 fruit
1 milk

CHOCOLATE-PEANUT BUTTER TREATS (page 145)

Ingredients	*Food Exchange Equivalents*
2/3 cup instant chocolate milk powder	2 milks
1/2 cup oatmeal	1 bread *or* cereal
2 Tbsp. peanut butter	2 proteins
1 tsp. vanilla	minimal caloric value
1/2 tsp. cinnamon	minimal caloric value
1 cup sugar-free applesauce	2 fruits
12 walnut halves	12 fats
2 Tbsp. raisins	1 fruit

Food Exchange Total: 2 milks
1 bread *or* cereal
2 proteins
3 fruits
12 fats

Appestoppers & Condiments

The road to good eating has many milestones. Appetizers and condiments are good places to start.

Appetizers can take the edge off your appetite—even slowing it down to a "stop" of sorts! They also make a refreshing entree to the main dish. Condiments are those extra little touches to make a meal special.

Do you hesitate to make time for them? If so, remember their flavors and colors can do wonders to enhance any meal. Romans 12:2 says:

Be a new and different person with a fresh newness in all you do and think. (TLB)

That word "new" comes up again. Does it also say to you, "Begin *now*"?

POINTERS TO HEALTHFUL EATING

Vegetable and fruit lovers should enjoy this section! If you haven't been the type to make a beeline for the fruit and vegetable stands on the country roads or at the supermarket, still try out these recipes. Give yourself a chance to appreciate the unusual flavors and the eye appeal vegetables and fruits have.

Remember that you can eat virtually unlimited amounts of non-starchy vegetables. Fruits are limited to *three* a day for women; *four* a day for men. Be aware of the protein amounts. Your noon protein portion is 2 ounces; your evening portion is 3-4 ounces.

APPETIZERS

Grapefruit-Shrimp Appetizer

shredded lettuce *or* curly endive
16 cooked shrimp
2 pink grapefruits, peeled and
  sectioned
1/2 cup chopped celery
8 tsp. low-cal French dressing

Place lettuce in four fancy sherbet glasses. Arrange shrimp, grapefruit, and celery on top. Drizzle 2 tsp. French dressing on each.

Shrimp-Vegetable Hors D'oeuvres

dash of celery powder
dash of garlic powder
1 tsp. vinegar
1/2 tsp. prepared mustard
1/2 tsp. horseradish
1/2 cup tomato juice
1 small can mushrooms, drained
1 small can shrimp, drained
1 small can water chestnuts, drained

In small saucepan, combine first 6 ingredients; cook about 5 minutes or until thickened. Marinate mushrooms in sauce. Meanwhile, slice chestnuts in half and salt lightly. Drain mushrooms. Place one shrimp, mushroom, and chestnut on each toothpick.

Cheez Dip

Base:
1 cup cottage cheese
2 oz. Muenster *or* Swiss cheese
dash of salt
milk

Blend all ingredients until smooth. Add milk to thin if needed.

Variations:

Dill Pickle Dip: To *Base*, add 1 chopped dill pickle.

Chive or Pimiento Dip: To *Base*, add 1 Tbsp. chives, pimiento, or parsley.

Garlic Dip: To *Base*, add 1/4 tsp. garlic powder, 1/4 tsp. paprika, dash of chili powder, 1 tsp. Worcestershire sauce.

Chive Dip

1 cup 99% fat-free cottage cheese
2 Tbsp. chicken bouillon
4 Tbsp. water
1 Tbsp. finely chopped parsley
1 Tbsp. chopped chives
1/2 tsp. dill

Whip cheese, bouillon, and water in blender until creamy. Stir in remaining ingredients. Chill at least 1 hour before serving.

Horseradish Dip

1 cup 99% fat-free cottage cheese
1 Tbsp. horseradish
1/4 tsp. dry mustard
2 drops Worcestershire sauce
2 drops hot pepper sauce

Combine all ingredients. Using high speed on mixer or blender, beat until smooth.

Onion Dip

8 oz. low-fat cottage cheese
1 pkg. onion seasoning
1 tsp. Worcestershire sauce
1 tsp. lemon juice
parsley flakes for color

Put all ingredients in blender or use mixer until smooth. Add a little skim milk if too thick. Chill. Serve with lots of raw vegetables.

Alpha Eckstein

Spicy Dip

1/4 cup tomato juice
1/4 cup mustard relish
1 Tbsp. horseradish
1 Tbsp. Worcestershire sauce
dash of cayenne
salt and pepper to taste
Italian spices

Combine all ingredients thoroughly and adjust seasonings to taste. Chill. Dip in raw vegetables. Makes about 3/4 cup.

Spinach Dip

1 10-oz. pkg. frozen chopped spinach
2 cups plain yogurt
1 cup chopped fresh parsley
1 1/2 Tbsp. lemon juice
1/2 cup minced green onion
1 Tbsp. dried dill weed
1/4 tsp. dried tarragon
1/4 tsp. dried chives
1/4 tsp. thyme
1 tsp. salt

Thaw, drain, and wring spinach in paper towels. Combine remaining ingredients and stir in spinach. Cover and refrigerate 24 hours. Serve with raw broccoli, cauliflower, green pepper, radishes, and carrot sticks. Makes 3 cups.

Vegetable Dip

1 carton low-fat yogurt
1/2 pkg. powdered salad dressing mix

Chill and serve with raw finger vegetables.

CONDIMENTS: JAMS AND ASSOCIATES

Apple Jelly

2 envelopes unflavored gelatin
1 qt. unsweetened apple juice *or* cider
2 Tbsp. lemon juice
2 Tbsp. sweetener
2 drops yellow food coloring
2 drops red food coloring

In saucepan, soften gelatin, apple and lemon juices, stirring well to dissolve. Bring to a boil; stir while boiling for 1 minute. Remove from heat and stir in liquid sweetener and food coloring. Pour into hot, sterilized half-pint jars, seal well, and place in refrigerator for 5 hours or overnight before using. Keep stored in refrigerator. Keeps for up to 3 weeks. Makes 4 half-pints.

Apple Butter

3 lbs. apples, peeled, cored, and
   sliced
1/2 cup water
1 cup vinegar
5 Tbsp. sweetener
6 tsp. cinnamon
1/4 tsp. cloves
1/8 tsp. ginger

Cook apples until soft; mash. Combine all ingredients and cook together for 45 minutes, stirring often. Cool. Makes 1 quart.

Orange-Pineapple Marmalade

1 orange
4 oz. frozen unsweetened orange-
   pineapple juice thawed
dash of salt
1 envelope unflavored gelatin

Wash orange and grate rind. Mix rind with juice. Peel orange and break into small pieces. Set aside. Put gelatin into large pan. Add orange juice and stir. Bring to a boil; then remove from heat. Add orange sections. Refrigerate. Makes 1 cup.

Pineapple-Rhubarb Jam

8 cups cut-up rhubarb
sweetener to equal 6 cups sugar
1 cup crushed pineapple
2 envelopes dietetic strawberry
   gelatin

Combine rhubarb and sweetener, letting stand overnight. Boil 4 min-

utes. Add crushed pineapple and bring to a boil. Remove from heat. Sprinkle gelatin on top. Stir and pour into jars.

Strawberry Jam

1/4 cup lemon juice
1 envelope unflavored gelatin
1 tsp. sweetener
2 cups strawberries, washed and
   hulled

In medium saucepan, mix together lemon juice and gelatin until smooth. Then add sweetener and strawberries, stirring constantly. Heat to full boil; boil for 3 minutes. Remove from heat and pour into jars. Cool and refrigerate.

CONDIMENTS: PICKLED FOODS

Bread and Butter Pickles

1 qt. thinly sliced cucumbers
2 Tbsp. salt
1 tray ice cubes
2 cups white vinegar
32 drops sweetener
1/2 tsp. turmeric
1/2 tsp. celery seed
water

Combine cucumbers, salt, and ice cubes. Let stand 1 hour. Combine remaining ingredients to make 4 cups liquid. Add cucumbers and bring to a fast boil. Turn heat to simmer until cucumbers lose bright green color. Place in glass container and refrigerate.

Variation: Add red pepper chunks and a small diced onion.

Cucumber Pickles

6 firm cucumbers, washed and dried
1/4 cup salt
1 1/2 Tbsp. sweetener
1/4 cup water
2 cups white vinegar
2 Tbsp. mixed pickling spices
pint jars

Cut cucumbers into sticks to fit pint jars. Place in large bowl, sprinkle with salt, and let stand overnight. Rinse and drain well several times. Combine sweetener, water, and vinegar in large kettle; bring to a boil. Add pickling spices (tied in a cheesecloth bag) and cucumbers. Reduce heat and simmer for 15 minutes. Pack into clean, hot pint jars. Heat liquid again to boiling; pour over cucumbers in jars. Seal at once.

Pickled Carrots

1 lb. carrots, cooked to crisp
garlic wine vinegar
liquid sweetener
celery seed
mustard seed
turmeric
cinnamon, cloves, nutmeg, ginger
salt and pepper to taste

Combine all ingredients, using seasonings with a light hand and adjust to taste. This may be canned or will keep several weeks in the refrigerator.

Variation: It's a great marinade for fish *or* meats. Marinate overnight before serving or at least several hours.

Pickled Dilly Eggs

12 hard-cooked eggs, shelled
1 medium onion, sliced
3/4 cup water
1 1/2 cups white vinegar
1 tsp. salt
1 tsp. dill weed
1 clove garlic, minced
1/2 tsp. mustard seed

Pack eggs and onion slices alternately in a 1-qt. jar. In pan, bring remaining ingredients to a boil; reduce heat and simmer 5-7 minutes. Pour over eggs and cover. Seal and chill at least 3 days. Will keep 2-3 weeks refrigerated. Each egg is 1 oz. of protein.

Dilled Vegetable Pickles

1 tsp. lightly crushed dill seed
1/4 cup vinegar
1 tsp. salt
sweetener to equal 1 tsp. sugar
dash of hot pepper sauce
1 cup water
2 cups raw vegetables of your choice
2 Tbsp. finely chopped pimiento

Combine first six ingredients in saucepan. Bring to a boil; while liquid is still hot, pour over vegetables. Cool; add pimiento and chill at least 24 hours. Drain; then cover and store in refrigerator.

Vegetable Pickles

1 cup white vinegar
1 cup water
sugar substitute to equal 3/4 cup sugar
1 large clove garlic, halved
dash of salt
1 lb. green beans *or* brussels sprouts
  or broccoli
2 pint jars, sterilized

Bring all ingredients, except vegetables, to a boil. Pack vegetables in pint jars. Pour hot brine over, leaving 1/4" on top. Cover. Will keep in refrigerator 3 weeks.

Pickled Mushrooms

2/3 cup tarragon vinegar
2 Tbsp. salad oil
1 clove garlic, crushed
2 drops sweetener
2 Tbsp. water
1 1/2 tsp. salt
dash of fresh pepper
dash of bottled hot pepper sauce
1 medium onion, sliced
12 oz. fresh *or* canned mushrooms

Combine ingredients. Cover and refrigerate.

Cucumber Refrigerator Pickles

2-3 large cucumbers, sliced
1 medium onion, thinly sliced
2 Tbsp. salt
1/4 cup white vinegar
2 1/2 Tbsp. sweetener

Cover cucumbers and onion with water; add salt. Let stand 2 hours. Drain; add vinegar and sweetener. Place in covered container. Will keep up to 3 months.

CONDIMENTS: *RELISHES; Fruit-based*

Cranberry Orange Relish

1 bag fresh cranberries, washed
1/2 orange, seeded
1/4 lemon, seeded
sweetener to taste

Process fruits in blender. Add sweetener; then chill.

Pineapple Relish

2 envelopes unflavored gelatin
1/2 cup cold water
1 16-oz. can crushed pineapple
sweetener to equal 1/4 cup sugar
dash of salt
3 Tbsp. lemon juice
1 cup chopped celery
1/4 cup chopped green pepper
2 pimientos, diced

In a bowl, mix gelatin with water. Drain juice from pineapple into a 2-cup measure; add water to make 2 cups. Heat to boiling; stir into gelatin mixture until dissolved. Stir in remaining ingredients except vegetables; chill to egg white consistency. Fold in vegetables and fruit. Mold or place in empty aluminum cans until firm. Cut out both ends; unmold and slice.

Note: This makes a great turkey or chicken accompaniment or a nice gift if you wrap the can with colorful paper or foil.

Three-Fruit Cranberry Relish

1 1/2 cups crushed pineapple
1 pkg. cranberries
20 drops sweetener
1 orange, sectioned

Place crushed pineapple and half pkg. cranberries in blender. Blend slowly until well chopped. Remove from blender and set aside. Place remaining cranberries, sweetener, and orange sections in blender; process until well chopped. Mix all ingredients together and chill.

CONDIMENTS: RELISHES; Vegetable-based

Beet Relish

1 cup chopped beets
1 cup chopped cabbage
sweetener to equal 1 cup sugar
horseradish to taste

Place ingredients in saucepan and just cover with vinegar. Boil 5 minutes and pack into jars.

Cucumber Relish

1 large cucumber
1 oz. onion, diced
1 1/2 tsp. lemon juice
3 Tbsp. parsley flakes
salt and pepper to taste
grated lemon peel to taste

Peel and cut cucumber in half lengthwise. Scoop out seeds, grate cucumber, and drain thoroughly. Combine with onion, lemon juice, and parsley flakes. Season with salt and pepper. Add grated lemon peel to taste. Refrigerate before serving over fish or salad.

Farmland Cabbage Relish

4 cups finely chopped cabbage
1/2 cup finely chopped green pepper
1/2 cup cider vinegar
sweetener to taste
1/2 cup water
2 tsp. salt

In a large bowl, mix all ingredients together. Let stand at least one hour. Cover and refrigerate; it stays fresh for several weeks. Drain well before serving.

Green Pickle Relish

1 qt. non-garlic dill pickles
1 tsp. minced, flaked dry onions
sweetener to taste

Rinse pickles well and grind up. Sprinkle with onion flakes; add sweetener to taste. Place in small saucepan. Bring to a boil and simmer. Delicious in tuna salad!

Hot Green Chili Relish

6 fresh jalapeño peppers, chopped
2 bell peppers, chopped
2 bunches green onions, chopped
6 tomatoes, diced
1 jar picante sauce
1/2 tsp. garlic salt
1 tsp. savory salt
1 Tbsp. salad oil
3 Tbsp. vinegar
1 tsp. coarse black pepper
salt to taste

Mix all ingredients and chill. This recipe is hot. Use it sparingly to enhance the flavor of eggs, beef, poultry, fish, and vegetables.

Margot Purdy

Red Cabbage Relish

2 Tbsp. water
1/4 cup chopped raw onion
1 small head red cabbage, shredded
1/4 cup red wine vinegar
4 Tbsp. raisins
1 tsp. salt

In skillet with water, sauté onion until tender. Stir in cabbage, wine vinegar, raisins, and salt. Cook over low heat until tender. Serve hot or cold.

Sweet Cabbage Relish

4 cups finely chopped cabbage
6-8 green peppers, finely chopped
1/4 cup instant onion flakes
1/2 cup coarse pickling salt
sweetener equal to 3 cups *or* to taste
2 cups vinegar

1 cup water
1 Tbsp. celery seed
2 Tbsp. mustard seed
green food coloring

Combine cabbage, green pepper, onion flakes, and pickling salt. Mix and let stand overnight in a plastic bowl or crock. Rinse well and drain. Make syrup by combining remaining ingredients. Then, combine vinegar mixture and relish vegetables; simmer for 15 minutes. Eat hot or cooled. Store in refrigerator. Makes about 4 pints or 2 quarts.

Tomato Relish

2 28-oz. cans tomatoes, chopped and drained
1 small onion, chopped
1 stalk celery, finely chopped
1/4 cup vinegar
1/4 tsp. mustard seed
1/4 tsp. celery seed
1/4 tsp. salt
1/4 tsp. pepper

In heavy pan, combine all ingredients and bring to a boil. Simmer 25-30 minutes, stirring often. Measure into hot jars. Keeps 3 weeks in refrigerator. Great meat accompaniment.

Vegetable Relish

10 medium green peppers, washed and seeded
1 lb. *or* 1/2 medium head cabbage, washed
1 lb. carrots, scraped and sliced
1 lb. onions

3 cups white vinegar
1/2 cup water
3 Tbsp. sweetener
3 Tbsp. kosher salt
1 Tbsp. mustard seed
1 Tbsp. celery seed

Quarter green peppers, and trim cabbage; peel and quarter onions. Put all vegetables through coarse blade of food chopper or blender. Drain well. Combine with remaining ingredients in large kettle. Bring to a boil; reduce heat and simmer about 5 minutes. Pack into clean and hot pint jars. Seal at once. Makes 6 pints.

Soups

Soup "sticks to the stomach," "warms a winter day," and "makes you feel better when you're down." These old-timey phrases about soup make good sense. Especially if the soup is homemade!

Despite the appealing ads from Messrs. Campbell and Heinz, homemade soup still captures the best flavor and texture. A pot of your own stock and chopped vegetables can satisfy as no canned soup can.

Preparing your own stock and vegetables, along with enjoying the aroma of soup simmering, can be therapy in itself! Large quantities of soup can be frozen in smaller containers for future use. In this way, you'll also have extra soup on hand to give to a friend or neighbor during illness. 2 Corinthians 1:3, 4 reminds us how wonderful God is:

He is the Father of our Lord Jesus Christ, the source of every mercy, and the one who so wonderfully comforts and strengthens us in our hardships and trials . . . so that when others are troubled, needing our sympathy and encouragement, we can pass on to them this same help and comfort God has given us! (TLB)

Refresh your spirit and someone else's today. Make a pot of soup and share it!

POINTERS TO HEALTHFUL EATING

Vegetables are the main ingredients in our soups. For a good reason—they're generally so low in calories! Do keep in mind the protein amounts: 2 ounces of meat, chicken, fish, or cheese at noon; 3-4 ounces in the evening.

Try making a meal of soup—not just the prelude to an eating event. Garnishing soup is one way to make it look special and inviting. Appearances do make a difference—even with foods! Try the following *Soup Surprises:*

To make light or clear soups look rich, float lemon slices, cucumber rounds, snipped chives, or sliced olives.

Glamorize creamed soups with sieved hard-cooked egg yolk.

Other pleasant additions to soups and foods are the following *Herbs*, *Spices*, and *Vegetable* garnishes and seasonings:

Herbs:

anise:	bisques, borscht, cabbage, cucumber, fish, mushrooms
basil:	broths, cheese, green peas, tomatoes, vegetables, minestrone
mint:	cucumber, fish, fresh green peas
oregano:	fish, peas, mushrooms, tomatoes, vegetables, beef, bisques, broths, chicken, onions
rosemary:	bisques, chicken, fish, peas, minestrone
sage:	bisques, bouillabaisse, fish, peas, tomatoes
savory:	beef, beets, cabbage, vegetables
tarragon:	asparagus, bisques, chicken, fish, peas
thyme:	beef, bisques, bouillabaisse, fish, peas, tomatoes

Spices:

allspice:	beef bisques, fish, green pea and tomato soups
caraway:	borscht, fish and cream soups
celery seed:	chicken, fish, and vegetable
chili powder:	avocado, tomatoes
cloves:	beef, green peas, tomatoes, vegetables
curry;	asparagus, chicken, fish, tomatoes
fennel:	borscht, cabbage, creams, fish
nutmeg:	beef bisques, chicken, cucumber, fish, fruits, and vegetables
poppy seed:	all soups and creams
saffron:	bouillabaisse, chicken, fish
sesame seed:	creams

Vegetables:

carrot:	grated
celery:	sliced, diced or chopped, including leaves
mushrooms:	finely chopped
chive:	minced
cucumbers:	unpeeled, thinly sliced
cress:	minced, whole sprigs
shallots:	thinly sliced, white or green
spinach:	minced
parsley:	minced, whole sprigs
green peppers:	chopped, diced, sliced in thin strips
radishes:	thinly sliced

SOUPS

Noble Borscht (Beet Soup)

1 large can sliced beets (no sugar added)
1 1/2 cans water
2-3 tsp. lemon juice
salt and pepper
chicken giblets
2 tsp. sweetener
1 clove garlic or 1/2 tsp. garlic powder
1 small onion

Cook ingredients together about 1/2 hour or until chicken giblets are tender. The sweet and sour taste is delicious with cooked and drained shredded cabbage.

Cabbage Soup

1 large can tomato juice
3-4 chicken bouillon cubes
1 can bean sprouts
1/2 or 1 head cabbage, shredded
2 cans French-style green beans
1 can mushrooms
2 stalks celery, chopped

Combine all ingredients and simmer together 3-4 hours.

Variation: Add other vegetables.

Caribbean Pumpkin Soup

2 1/2 cups mashed pumpkin, drained
3 cups chicken broth or bouillon
1 small onion, chopped or diced very fine
pepper
1 cup skim milk
1/2 Tbsp. curry powder
dried or fresh mint leaves

In saucepan, combine pumpkin and broth to make a thin puree. Simmer onion in a non-stick skillet until soft. Add onion to puree and boil for 3 minutes. Add pepper, milk, and curry powder. Heat through, stirring constantly. Sprinkle with mint before serving.

Note: Use either fresh or canned pumpkin. If using fresh, cook in small amount of water until pumpkin is soft; then drain well.

Cream of Broccoli Soup

1 cup beef bouillon
2 cups skim milk
1/2 cup instant milk powder
dash of garlic powder
salt and pepper to taste
2 cups cooked, chopped broccoli

Gently heat broth, skim milk, milk powder, and seasonings. Do not allow to boil. Add broccoli; let stand a few minutes and serve. Makes 4 cups.

Variation: For a full-meal soup, add 3 oz. grated Muenster cheese and stir until melted. Serve with whole wheat toast.

Cream of Cauliflower Soup

6 cups water
1 pkg. frozen cauliflower
1/2 cup chopped onions
1 Tbsp. celery
1 Tbsp. chopped parsley
2 cloves garlic, chopped
salt and pepper to taste
1 Tbsp. margarine
2 cups skim milk
1 Tbsp. flour
2 Tbsp. grated Parmesan cheese

Cook vegetables in water. Add both to blender and process until smooth. In another pot, sauté seasonings in margarine. Add blended vegetables and cook 20 minutes. Place skim milk, flour, and cheese in blender. Blend 30 seconds and add to soup. Cook uncovered 20 to 30 minutes.

Variation: Use chopped broccoli or spinach, instead of cauliflower.

Cheryl Doyle

Cream of Celery Soup

3 1/2 cups chicken broth *or* bouillon
1 small onion, minced
3 cups finely chopped celery
salt and pepper to taste
2 Tbsp. flour
3 Tbsp. water
1 1/2 cups evaporated skim milk *or*
   1 cup dry milk powder *and*
   1 cup water

Bring broth to a boil. Add onion, celery, and seasonings. Cover and simmer over low heat until tender but slightly crisp. Gradually pour in milk or milk powder liquid. Make a

thickening of flour and water, and fold into soup. Cook 5-10 minutes, stirring occasionally. Makes 6 cups. This is great with a veggie sandwich on pita bread!

Cream of Mushroom Soup #1

1 1/2 cups chopped onion
3 cups chopped mushroom stems
1 tsp. margarine *or* sweet butter
6 cups hot water *or* stock
2 cups diced potatoes
3 cups sliced mushroom caps
2 cups instant milk powder
2 tsp. salt
1/2 tsp. paprika
1/4 cup freshly chopped *or* 3 Tbsp.
   dried parsley

Sauté onions and mushroom stems in margarine. Stir in 1 cup water or stock and simmer 15 minutes. Place in blender and process until smooth. Set puree aside. Put 2 Tbsp. water or stock into pan. Add potatoes and sauté for about 7 minutes, stirring occasionally. Stir in puree and remaining stock or water. Bring to a boil, lower heat, and simmer 15 minutes stirring when needed. Add sliced mushrooms. Make paste from milk powder and small amount of water. Add to soup, along with salt, paprika, and parsley. Heat through and serve. Makes 3 quarts. Makes 8 portions at 100 calories per serving.

Cream of Mushroom Soup #2

1 can mushrooms, drained
1/2 cup skim milk

1/4 cup water
1/2 pkg. frozen cauliflower, thawed
dash of dried parsley
dash of paprika

Put 1/2 can mushrooms, milk, water, and cauliflower in blender; process until smooth. Pour into medium saucepan. Add remaining mushrooms. Heat until boiling. Add parsley and paprika. Makes 1 serving.

Cream of Vegetable Soup #1

1 1/2 cups chicken broth
1/2 cup chopped onion
desired vegetable and seasonings
  (see chart below)
2 Tbsp. sweet butter or margarine
2 Tbsp. flour
1/2 tsp. salt

pinch of white pepper
1 cup milk, preferably skim

In saucepan, combine chicken broth, onion, and one of the vegetable-seasoning combinations from the chart. Bring to boiling. Reduce heat; cover and simmer according to chart or until vegetable is tender. (Remove bay leaf if using broccoli). Place vegetable mixture in a blender container or food processor. Cover and blend 30 to 60 seconds or until smooth. In same saucepan, melt butter or margarine. Blend in flour, salt, and pepper. Add milk all at once. Cook and stir until thickened and bubbly. Stir in vegetable puree. Cook until heated through for a warm soup. For a chilled soup, cover and refrigerate for several hours.

VEGETABLE	SEASONINGS	TIMING	YIELD
2 cups broccoli, cut up	1/2 tsp. dried thyme, crushed 1 small bay leaf dash of garlic powder	10 minutes	3 1/2 cups
1 cup sliced carrots	1 Tbsp. snipped parsley 1/2 tsp. dried basil, crushed	12 minutes	3 1/2 cups
1 1/2 cups cut green beans	1/2 tsp. dried savory, crushed	20 to 30 minutes	3 cups
1 1/2 cups shelled peas	1/4 cup shredded lettuce 2 Tbsp. chopped ham 1/4 tsp. dried sage, crushed	8 minutes	3 1/2 cups
1 cup sliced potatoes	1/2 tsp. dried dillweed	10 minutes	3 cups

Cream of Vegetable Soup #2

leftover green beans, peas, or
   asparagus
1 Tbsp. parsley
several celery tops
1/3 cup instant milk powder
2 cups chicken bouillon

Process vegetables and milk powder in blender until smooth. Add chicken bouillon. Heat and serve.

Curried Chicken Soup

12 cups cold chicken broth,
   fat-skimmed
2 Tbsp. curry powder
1/4 tsp. Tabasco sauce
1 cup white wine vinegar
salt and pepper to taste
4 sour green apples, cooked and
   pureed
finely chopped chives
finely chopped parsley
2 cups evaporated skim milk
paprika

Combine all, but last two, ingredients. Heat and adjust seasonings to taste. Serve hot or cold. Before serving, add hot or cold milk; stir well and sprinkle with paprika.

Egg Drop Soup #1

1 tsp. onion flakes
1 1/2 cups water
1/2 tsp. caraway seeds
1 chicken bouillon cube
1 egg, slightly beaten

Simmer first 4 ingredients for 15 minutes. Strain hot broth and discard seeds and onion. Return broth to a boil; slowly pour in egg from a cup and briskly stir the broth. Serve immediately. Makes 1 serving.

Egg Drop Soup #2

4 cups chicken broth or bouillon
salt to taste
dash of ginger
1 Tbsp. minced green onions
2 Tbsp. sliced mushrooms
1 egg, slightly beaten

Bring all ingredients, except egg, to a boil. Add egg to boiling soup. Stir until egg shreds. Serve immediately.

French Onion Soup

4 cups water
16 oz. fresh onion, peeled and diced
4 beef bouillon cubes
salt to taste
grated Swiss or Parmesan cheese

In a saucepan, simmer onions, bouillon, and water until tender. Add salt. Pour heated soup into 4 bowls. Top with grated Swiss or Parmesan cheese or a little of both. Go easy on the cheese.

Minestrone

3 cups water
3 beef bouillon cubes
1 stalk celery, diced
1 carrot, diced
1 tomato, diced
1 onion, chopped
pinch of thyme

grated Muenster or Swiss cheese
1 Tbsp. chopped parsley
1/2 cup shredded cabbage
1/4 tsp. savory
1 bay leaf
salt and pepper to taste

Combine water and bouillon in pot. Add remaining ingredients, except cheese, and bring to a boil. Simmer for 45 minutes or until tender. Sprinkle with 1/2 oz. cheese per serving. Makes 4 portions at 25 calories each.

Mock Chicken-Noodle Soup

4 chicken bouillon cubes
4 cups water
6 stalks celery
1/4 tsp. pepper
2 Tbsp. parsley flakes

Combine bouillon cubes and water. Cut celery into paper-thin strips, and add to bouillon with pepper and parsley flakes. Simmer for about 30 minutes over low heat until celery resembles noodles.

Oh-Ho Soup

3 cups beef bouillon
1 cup tomato juice
2 Tbsp. soy sauce
3 Tbsp. vinegar
1/4 tsp. pepper
1/4 cup chopped string beans

Combine all ingredients. Bring to a boil. Simmer about 10 minutes. Makes 4 servings.

Mint Soup

2 onions, sliced
cooking oil
4 tomatoes, quartered
1/4 cup mint leaves, washed
1/2 cup chicken stock or bouillon
salt to taste
cayenne pepper to taste
1 egg yolk
1 tsp. vinegar
1/2 cup grated Swiss cheese

Sauté onions in small amount of oil until golden. Add tomatoes, mint leaves, stock, salt, and pepper; cook for 15 minutes. Pass soup through a food mill. Mix egg yolk with vinegar in bottom of a soup tureen. Pour soup into the tureen, stirring continuously with a wooden spoon. Serve with grated cheese.

Pepper Pot Soup

6 chicken bouillon cubes
5 cups boiling water
1 bay leaf
1 tsp. salt
1 tsp. pepper
1/8 tsp. thyme
1 tsp. onion salt
1 cup chopped green peppers
1 cup chopped celery

Dissolve bouillon cubes in boiling water. Add remaining ingredients. Cover and simmer about 30 minutes. Makes 6 servings.

Mock Pea Soup

3 cups water
6 stalks celery, diced
6 sprigs parsley
1 onion bouillon cube
1 16-oz. can asparagus
mace to taste
bay leaf to taste
salt and pepper to taste

Blend all ingredients in blender. Bring to a boil and simmer for 30 minutes.

Rice and Bean Soup

1 Tbsp. oil
1 1/2 cups chopped onions
2 tsp. garlic powder
1 cup chopped carrots
1 cup chopped celery
1 cup diced potatoes
7-8 cups shredded cabbage
8 cups water
4 chicken bouillon cubes
1 cup tomato juice
1/2 cup freshly chopped or 1/4 cup dried parsley
1 bay leaf
salt to taste
1 tsp. thyme
1/2 cup cooked soybeans, drained
3/4 cup cooked brown rice
3 tomatoes, chopped
3/4 cup yogurt or grated cheese or cottage cheese

Heat oil, and sauté onions, garlic powder, carrots, celery, and potatoes for about 10 minutes until potatoes are translucent. Stir in cabbage and cook until soft. Stir in water and bouillon cubes, seasonings, soybeans, and rice. Bring to a boil and simmer 1/2 hour. Just before serving, stir in chopped tomatoes. Top each cup of soup with 2 Tbsp. yogurt. Makes 2 1/2 quarts. Serves around 6 at 150 calories per serving.

String Bean Soup

2 lbs. string beans, cut up
2 qts. water
salt to taste
2 tsp. chopped parsley
1 small onion, chopped
1 Tbsp. flour
1/4 cup cold water
1/2 tsp. paprika
1 Tbsp. vinegar
1/4 cup instant milk powder

In large kettle, bring beans, water, salt, and parsley to a boil. Simmer until beans are tender. In small pan, cook onion in 1 Tbsp. water. Add flour and cook, stirring until slightly browned. Stir in cold water and paprika. Stir this mixture into beans; add vinegar. Heat and add milk powder. Makes approximately 10 cups.

Super Easy Soup

1 cup water
1 bouillon cube
1 tsp. chives
1 tsp. parsley flakes
1 Tbsp. chopped celery or Chinese cabbage

Combine all ingredients in a saucepan; bring just to a boil. Makes 1 serving. Serve.

Tomato Soup

1 small can stewed tomatoes
1/2 cup cooked carrots, fresh or canned
1/2 tsp. onion powder
1 beef bouillon cube
2 drops sweetener
pinch of basil
1/3 cup instant milk powder
salt and pepper to taste

Combine all ingredients; blend well and heat. Makes 1 serving.

Vegetable Soup

cabbage, cut in chunks
cauliflower flowerettes
chopped celery
chopped Chinese cabbage
diced green pepper
chopped parsley
chopped chives
garlic powder
salt and pepper to taste
3 cups chicken bouillon
1 cup tomato juice

Use vegetables in amounts desired; cook with seasonings in water to almost cover. Add bouillon and tomato juice; simmer 30 minutes.

Beef-Vegetable Soup

3 cups water
1 cup canned, medium tomatoes
1/2 cup chopped celery
1/3 cup sliced carrots
2 oz. chopped onion
2 beef bouillon cubes
1 clove garlic, minced
1/8 tsp. pepper
1 lb. ground beef cooked and crumbled

In a 4-qt. saucepan or slow cooker, combine all ingredients except beef. Bring to a boil. Reduce and simmer, covered, about 10 minutes. Add beef; simmer 10 to 15 minutes longer or until heated throughout. Makes 4 servings.

Chicken-Vegetable Soup

1 chicken breast
1 1/2 qts. water
1 large onion, chopped
2 stalks celery with leaves
1 large zucchini, diced
1 large carrot, diced
1 1/2 tsp. basil
1 tsp. salt
2 cups canned tomatoes
1 small parsnip or turnip
1 cup peas or green beans
bouquet garni—made by tying the following in cheesecloth:
    3 sprigs parsley
    1 large bay leaf
    6 whole peppercorns
    2 whole cloves

Cook chicken breast in 2 cups water until very tender. Cool and cut up into small pieces. Chill broth until fat rises to top and skim off. In pan, sauté onion, celery, zucchini, carrot, and basil in 2 Tbsp. water until tender; keep stirring. Add other ingredients and bring to a boil over medium heat. Reduce heat, cover, and simmer 1 1/2 hours.

Vegetable-Rice Soup

5 cups chicken bouillon
1/3 cup uncooked rice
1/4 tsp. onion powder
1 small carrot, thinly sliced
2/3 cup fresh or frozen peas
1/8 tsp. dry mustard
2 cups chopped cauliflower
1 small onion, minced
1/4 cup chopped celery
salt and pepper to taste
1 cup skim milk
3 oz. grated cheese

In a medium pan, heat broth to a boil; add all ingredients, except milk and cheese. Cover and simmer over low heat until vegetables are tender. Add milk and cheese, stirring constantly until cheese is melted. Makes 8 cups at less than 100 calories per cup.

CHOWDERS:

Bouillabaisse (*Fish Chowder*)

1 Tbsp. olive oil
1/2 cup chopped onion
1 Tbsp. chopped garlic
1/2 cup chopped celery
1 1-lb. can stewed tomatoes
1 8-oz. can tomato juice
1 tsp. salt
1 Tbsp. paprika
3 cups water
basil
1 1/2 lbs. medium or large shrimp
3 sea bass or halibut steaks

1 lb. crabmeat
4 medium lobster tails
1 lb. clams or scallops, *optional*

Put all ingredients, except seafood, in slow cooker. Cover and cook on high for 2-4 hours. Add seafoods, cover, and cook for 1-3 hours on high.

Charlie's Fish Chowder

4 oz. chopped onion
1 tsp. margarine
1 tsp. garlic powder
dash of oregano
dash of basil
dash of thyme
3 oz. chopped celery
6 oz. stewed tomatoes, finely chopped
1 lb. boneless fish
1 1/2 qts. water
2 chicken bouillon cubes
salt and pepper to taste

Sauté onions in margarine and garlic powder. Add oregano, basil, and thyme; cook one minute. Add celery, tomatoes, and fish. Cook and stir about an hour, stirring frequently to keep from burning. Let cook down well. Add water and bouillon cubes, salt, and pepper to taste. Simmer and cook 1/2 hour without cover and 1 hour with cover. Remove any oils on surface.

Easy Fish Chowder

1 cup coarsely chopped carrots
1 tomato, cut up

3/4 cup chopped onion
1 cup water
1/2 cup chopped celery
1 bay leaf
1 green pepper, chopped
1 tsp. chopped parsley
1 12-oz. pkg. frozen cod, thawed
1/3 cup instant milk powder

In saucepan, place all ingredients, except cod and milk. Bring to a boil and simmer 15 minutes. Add fish and simmer 15 minutes more until fish flakes. Let cook down. Add milk powder and heat.

Variation: Add other vegetables, if desired.

Manhattan Clam Chowder

1 Tbsp. dry onion flakes
1 stalk celery, chopped
1/2 cup tomato juice
1/2 cup water
1 small bay leaf
salt and pepper to taste
4 oz. minced clams and juice
2 oz. chopped onion
2 oz. grated carrot

Simmer all ingredients, except clams, onion, and carrot, for 15 minutes. Add minced clams and juice. Heat and serve. Garnish with onion and grated carrot.

Tuna Chowder

1 chicken bouillon cube
1 cup water
soy sauce
3 3/4 oz. tuna fish

dash of parsley
1/4 cup mushrooms
1/2 tsp. chopped pimiento
1/2 cup French-style green beans
1/2 cup sliced asparagus

Heat bouillon cube, water, and soy sauce. Add tuna and vegetables. Serve hot.

Note: Add vegetable amounts as desired.

Hearty Turkey Chowder

8 cups turkey broth, fat skimmed*
1 lb. freshly ground turkey meat
1 tsp. salt
1/8 tsp. pepper
2 eggs
1 Tbsp. grated onion
1 slice bread, crumbed
1/2 cup skim milk
1/2 cup yogurt
1/2 cup water
2 Tbsp. lemon juice
2 Tbsp. chopped parsley

*Skim the fat from the broth by chilling it until the fat floats to the top.

Combine turkey, salt, pepper, eggs, onion, bread crumbs, and milk in a bowl. Shape the mixture into 36 small meatballs. In a pan, bring the broth to a boil. Add meatballs, cover, and simmer 10 minutes. Remove meatballs from broth and set them aside. Add yogurt to mixture, and continue cooking about 2 minutes until bubbly. Then add lemon juice and meatballs. Garnish with chopped parsley and serve.

Creamy Tuna-Broccoli Chowder

1 Tbsp. margarine
1 cup chopped onion
3 heaping Tbsp. arrowroot or 1 Tbsp. cornstarch
3 cups milk
1 10-oz. pkg. chopped broccoli
1 6-oz. can tuna, drained
2 Tbsp. chopped chives
1 1/2 tsp. salt
1/2 tsp. celery seed

Melt margarine. Sauté onion until tender. Stir in arrowroot or cornstarch. Gradually blend in milk. Cook over low heat, stirring constantly until soup bubbles and thickens slightly. Add remaining ingredients. Simmer covered for 5 minutes until broccoli is tender, but still slightly crisp. Serves 2.

Jan Steele

Chicken Chowder

1 chicken breast, boiled, boned, and skinned
1/2 cup diced cauliflower
8 oz. French-style green beans, cut fine
4 oz. peas
8 oz. summer squash, diced
1 Tbsp. onion flakes
2 Tbsp. arrowroot
3 cups water
2 chicken bouillon cubes
salt and pepper to taste

Dice chicken; place in saucepan, and add remaining ingredients. Bring to a boil; then simmer about 1 hour.

Charlene Bowen

Quick Clam Chowder

6 dozen (20 oz.) clams
1 cup clam broth, natural or canned
1 tsp. salt
1 tsp. white pepper
1/2 tsp. mace
1 tsp. imitation butter flavoring
1 qt. skim milk
2 Tbsp. chopped parsley

Place clams in a pot; cover with broth. Sprinkle with salt, pepper, and mace. Cover and simmer for 3 minutes. Add imitation butter flavoring to skim milk. Heat milk just to boiling. Place 1/4 of the clams in each of 4 bowls. Pour 1 cup of hot milk over each portion. Sprinkle with chopped parsley.

Vegetarian Chowder

2 cups (1 lb.) lentils, rinsed
2 1/2 qts. water
1 cup medium barley
1 Tbsp. oil
1 large onion, chopped
2 large ribs celery with leaves, chopped
1 large carrot, diced
1 large potato, pared and finely diced
3 Tbsp. minced parsley
1 16-oz. can tomatoes, cut up
3 tsp. salt
1/4 tsp. pepper

Remove any malformed lentils. Then combine all ingredients in a large kettle. Bring to a boil; reduce heat, cover, and simmer 1 hour until lentils and barley are tender. Add more water if mixture becomes too thick. Yields 4 quarts.

Variation: Add 1/2 cup uncooked rice and 1 1/2 cups water during last 1/2 hour of cooking.

Note: This recipe contains balanced protein portions and could be served as a one-dish meal.

Salads

Tossing together fruits and vegetables for a quick and filling salad is one way to get essential vitamins, minerals, and large amounts of cellulose or "fiber." Fiber helps keep our appetites satisfied and also absorbs water during the digestive process. Without fiber, digestive problems are a foregone conclusion!

Did you know that in Bible days vegetables and fruits were known for their health-producing qualities? Consider the example of Daniel and his three friends who requested a ten-day diet of vegetables and water:

... *at the end of the ten days, Daniel and his three friends looked healthier and better nourished than the youths who had been eating the food supplied by the king! So after that the steward fed them only vegetables and water, without the rich foods and wines!*   Daniel 1:15-16 (TLB)

POINTERS TO HEALTHFUL EATING

These salad and dressing recipes are good low-calorie versions. Most have omitted fats in the form of oils and mayonnaise. We suggest a maximum of 1 tablespoon of fat per day. Keep in mind that 1 teaspoon is equivalent to 35 calories. Restaurant dressings can contain 400-500 "hidden" calories, so think twice when you order a salad!

Experiment with the varieties of fruits and vegetables. Vegetable portions can be very large and still be low in calories.* Group A vegetables contain only about 25 calories; Group B vegetables have more natural sugar so that 1/2 cup is equivalent to 40 calories.

Again, be aware of the protein portions. We suggest 2 ounces at noon and 3-4 ounces in the evening.*

---

*Eat plenty of celery because celery contains fewer calories than it takes to chew it up. Theoretically if you eat enough, you'll disappear—careful not to overdo it!

FRUIT/VEGETABLE COMBOS

Cabbage-Apple Slaw

2 cups shredded red cabbage
1 apple, diced
1 tsp. mayonnaise
1 tsp. orange extract
1 Tbsp. skim milk
2 drops sweetener

Mix all ingredients together. Chill. Serves two.

Cottage Apple Slaw

2 cups shredded cabbage
1 medium apple, unpared, cored, and diced
1/2 cup dietetic blue-cheese dressing
1 1/2 cups cream-style cottage cheese

In a salad bowl, combine shredded cabbage and diced apple. Pour dressing over mixture; toss to coat. Spoon cottage cheese in ring around salad bowl. Makes 4 servings.

Fruity Cabbage Slaw

1 cup shredded cabbage
1 red apple, diced
1 cup thinly sliced red berries
1 cup undrained, crushed pineapple

Toss ingredients together lightly. Chill to marinate.

Pineapple Coleslaw

2 cups shredded cabbage
2 cups crushed pineapple
2 Tbsp. raisins
dash of salt

Combine all ingredients and chill well to marinate. Makes 3 servings.

Chinese Lotus Salad

1/4 lb. fresh young spinach leaves
1 naval orange, peeled and sectioned
4 oz. water chestnuts, drained and thinly sliced
1/4 cup vinegar
1 tsp. sweetener
2 Tbsp. soy sauce
1 can bean sprouts, drained

Trim spinach leaves. Wash and rinse several times. Fill salad bowl with leaves; arrange rows of orange sections and sliced water chestnuts on top. Chill. Mix together vinegar, sweetener, and soy sauce. Pour over salad just before serving.

Orange-Cucumber Salad

1/2 large cucumber, thinly sliced
1/4 tsp. salt
dash of pepper
2 medium oranges, pared and sectioned
1/2 cup chopped green pepper
2 Tbsp. snipped parsley
1/2 cup plain yogurt
1/4 tsp. dried thyme, crushed

In small mixing bowl, sprinkle cucumber with salt and pepper. Toss with orange, green pepper, and parsley. Combine yogurt and thyme; spoon onto salad mixture. Toss lightly to coat. Cover and chill.

Namasu

2 cucumbers, cut in half lengthwise
1 1/2 tsp. salt
2 oranges, halved lengthwise
2 stalks celery, diced
1/2 cup thinly sliced mushrooms
2 Tbsp. sugar
1/2 tsp. grated lemon peel
1/4 cup fresh lemon juice
1/4 cup white vinegar

Slice cucumbers thinly crosswise; place in a bowl and sprinkle with salt. Let stand 10 minutes. Rinse lightly; drain, gently squeezing out excess liquid. Peel oranges; make shallow V-shaped cut and remove center core. Cut into bite-sized pieces. Add oranges, celery, and mushrooms to cucumbers. In small bowl, mix remaining ingredients. Add to fruit and vegetables. Toss well, cover, and refrigerate. Serves 8.
Claudia Allen

Seven Wonder Salad

2 cups *or* 1/2 medium head cabbage
1/2 green pepper
1 tsp. pimiento
1/2 tsp. chives
1/2 tsp. parsley
2 stalks celery
1 Tbsp. mushrooms
3 radishes
1/2 cup French-style green beans, drained
1 small apple, cored and unpared
1/2 cup crushed pineapple
1/2 tsp. liquid sweetener
2 Tbsp. white vinegar

Finely chop or grate first 9 ingre-

dients. Put cored apple, pineapple, sweetener, and white vinegar in blender. Process until apple is well chopped. Mix salad and fruit mixtures together. Chill.

VEGETABLE SALADS

Bean Sprout Salad

3 cups bean sprouts
1 lb. can cut green beans, drained
1 lb. can wax beans, drained
1 lb. can red kidney beans, drained
   or 1 can chick-peas, drained
3/4 cup cider vinegar
1 Tbsp. oil
2 Tbsp. soy sauce
2 tsp. mustard
1 cup chopped onion
salt and pepper to taste

Put sprouts and beans in large bowl. Mix remaining ingredients and pour over beans. Toss well, cover, and marinate 3-4 hours in refrigerator. Makes 10-12 servings.

Blender Coleslaw

1 head cabbage, washed
salad dressing

Cut cabbage into 1" pieces; place in blender, and cover with cold water. Cover container and process 1 or 2 cycles at GRIND. Drain immediately in colander. Season and mix with mayonnaise or other salad dressing.

Note: Yogurt, mixed half and half with mayonnaise or slaw dressing, cuts the calories.

GROWING SPROUTS IN THE KITCHEN

We tested 31 sprouts. These 10 were winners!

LEAFY GREEN SPROUTS: in salads or as a garnish

	GROWING TIME	HARVEST SIZE	YIELD (Seeds)	(Sprouts)	TASTE
Alfalfa	3-5 days	1 1/2"-2"	1 Tbsp. makes 4 cups		crisp, mild, grassy
Chia	4-6 days	1 1/2"-2"	1 Tbsp. makes 2 cups		unique, full-bodied flavor
Garden cress	3-5 days	1 1/2"-2"	1 Tbsp. makes 2 cups		peppery, similar to water-cress, but milder
Mustard	5-6 days	1 1/2"-2"	1 Tbsp. makes 2 cups		pleasant bite, similar to mustard greens
Radish	2-5 days	1 1/2"-2"	1 Tbsp. makes 2 cups		hot radish flavor with older or infrequently watered plants

LARGER WHITE SPROUTS: in breads, entrees, salads

	GROWING TIME	HARVEST SIZE	YIELD (Seeds)	(Sprouts)	TASTE
Fenugreek	4-6 days	2"-3"	1 cup makes 12 cups		similar to mung but slightly bitter
Lentil	2-4 days	3/4"-1 1/2"	1 cup makes 6 cups		mildly spicy, fresh vegetable flavor and crunch, slightly starchy when raw
Mung bean	1-5 days (immature)	1/4" and up	1 cup makes 5-12 cups		pleasant legume flavor, crunchy
	5-7 days (commercial size)	2"-3"			
Rye	2 days	1/4"	1 cup makes 4 cups		similar to wheat but more subtle in flavor, less substantial
Wheat	2 days	1/4"	1 cup makes 4 cups		sweet, nutty, chewy, very filling

Materials needed:
large Mason jar
rubber band or metal ring cover
piece of cheesecloth, nylon stocking, or plastic screen
beans of choice

Directions:
First, soak beans (12 hours for wheat and mung beans; 2-3 hours for alfalfa).
Rinse and drain well. Place beans in jar. Put screen material over mouth of
jar, and secure with rubber band or metal ring cover. Place in a warm, dark,
dry place. Every 4-6 hours, rinse beans with cool-warm water (water temperature can affect whiteness of sprouts, so experiment!) and drain well. Let

sprouts grow to desired length and rinse thoroughly, carefully removing outer seed covering on large beans.

Note: A plastic screen lets rinse water drain well. If using a nylon stocking, rinse sprouts more often and take extra care in draining.

Oriental Coleslaw

1/4 head cabbage, shredded
2 cups alfalfa sprouts
1/4 cup chopped soybean sprouts
1/4 cup slivered green pepper
1 small onion, slivered
tart, low-cal coleslaw dressing

Combine vegetables together. Mix with dressing.

Twenty-Four Hour Coleslaw

12 cups chopped cabbage
1 medium onion, chopped
1/2 green pepper, chopped
2 1/4 cups vinegar and sweetener
  to equal 2 cups
1 Tbsp. or less salt
1 Tbsp. mustard seed
1 Tbsp. celery seed

In a large bowl, combine vegetables. Stir remaining ingredients together until mixed. Pour over vegetable mixture and toss well. Pack into jars or cover well. Chill at least 24 hours before serving. Makes 12 cups.

Variation: Use 1 1/2 unsweetened pineapple juice and 3/4 cup vinegar, instead of 2 1/4 cups vinegar and sweetener.

German Cucumbers in Oil and Vinegar

3 large cucumbers
1 medium onion
salt
garlic powder
1 Tbsp. oil
4 Tbsp. wine vinegar
freshly ground pepper

Wash, peel, and slice cucumbers and onion very thin. Layer them in bowl; sprinkle each layer liberally with salt and garlic powder. Let stand 3 hours; then drain off juice. Add oil, vinegar, and pepper to vegetables; marinate for an hour. Drain and serve, or chill before serving.

Shredded Cucumbers

2 cucumbers, peeled and shredded
1 tsp. salt
1/4 tsp. cayenne pepper
sweetener to equal 1/2 tsp. sugar
1 Tbsp. soy sauce
1 Tbsp. water
1/2 tsp. vinegar

Sprinkle cucumbers with salt. Let stand 1-2 hours; then drain. Combine remaining ingredients; pour over cucumbers and toss lightly. Serves 4.

Dorothy Spies

Hot Green Bean Salad

1/4 cup diet Italian salad dressing
2 9-oz. pkgs. frozen, cut green beans,
    partially thawed
1/2 cup sliced celery
1 large onion, sliced
2 tsp. dill

Combine salad dressing, green beans, and celery in a non-stick skillet. Cover and cook just until the beans are fully thawed, separating them with a fork as they cook. Then add the onion and dill; continue cooking for about 3 minutes. Stir occasionally until the vegetables are tender but still crisp. Makes 6 servings.

Three-Bean Salad

2 cups canned green beans
2 cups yellow wax beans
2 cups bean sprouts, rinsed and
    drained
1/2 cup thinly sliced onion
1/4 cup green pepper or pimiento
1/4 cup brown sugar substitute
1 tsp. celery salt
1/2 tsp. salt
1/2 tsp. black pepper
3/4 cup cider vinegar
1 tsp. Worcestershire sauce

Combine all ingredients in a large mixing bowl; cover and chill overnight. Drain well, toss slightly, and serve. Leftovers may be stored for several days in the refrigerator.

Sauerkraut Salad

1 large can sauerkraut
1/2 cup chopped mushrooms
1/2 cup chopped green pepper
1/2 cup chopped onion
1/2 cup chopped celery
1/2 cup chopped red pepper
Dressing

Drain sauerkraut thoroughly, and dry on paper towels. Layer all vegetables in a large bowl. Cover with *Dressing* and refrigerate 2-3 hours.

Dressing:
1/2 cup wine vinegar
1/4-1/2 cup sweetener
3 Tbsp. mustard
2 Tbsp. Worcestershire sauce
3 Tbsp. soy sauce
salt and pepper to taste

Place dressing ingredients in blender to mix.

Variation: Use pimiento instead of red pepper.

Spinach Salad #1

2 1/2 cups fresh spinach, cut up
10 fresh mushrooms, sliced
6 green onions, thinly sliced or
    1 small onion, finely diced
3 Tbsp. low-cal Italian dressing
1 tsp. sunflower seeds or almond
    slivers

Combine vegetables and toss with dressing. Top each serving with seeds or nuts. Makes 4 servings.

Spinach Salad #2

4 cups raw spinach, washed
2 cups sliced fresh mushrooms
1 medium onion, thinly sliced
1/4 cup low-cal Italian dressing
ground pepper to taste

Toss vegetables together well. Sprinkle with dressing and pepper; serve in individual bowls.

Variation: Top each serving with 1 tsp. bacon pieces, the soybean substitute kind.

Summer Garden Salad #1

1 cup peas, fresh *or* frozen
1 cup cut green beans, fresh *or* frozen
1 medium zucchini, washed and trimmed
1/2 medium cauliflower, washed
10-12 cherry tomatoes, halved
5-6 thinly sliced radishes
several leaves head lettuce, shredded
1/4 cup low-cal Italian dressing

Slightly cook peas and beans; drain, and cool. Thinly slice zucchini into salad bowl. Break cauliflower into small pieces. Add to bowl with tomatoes, radishes, and lettuce. Mix gently, adding peas and beans. Toss with dressing before serving. Serves 6-8.

Summer Garden Salad #2

4 drops sweetener
1/2 cup vinegar
salt and pepper to taste
1/4 cup chopped onion
1 green pepper, diced
1 cucumber, diced
3 cups leaf lettuce *or* head lettuce

Combine all ingredients, cover, and chill. Keeps one day in a covered dish.

Spring Salad Orientale

1 can fancy chow mein vegetables, drained
1 cup fresh bean *or* alfalfa sprouts
1 cup fresh snow pea pods
2 cups chopped fresh spinach
1 cup thinly sliced fresh mushrooms
low-cal Italian salad dressing to taste

Toss all ingredients together lightly.

Turnip Salad

3 oz. turnips, grated
1/2 cup thinly sliced Chinese cabbage
2 scallions, chopped
2 radishes, sliced paper thin
3 cups shredded romaine lettuce
1 Tbsp. wine vinegar
1/2 tsp. salt
1/4 tsp. black pepper
1/8 tsp. dry mustard
1/4 tsp. sweetener
1/4 tsp. dried basil, crushed

Combine turnips, cabbage, scallions, radishes, and lettuce in a salad bowl and chill. Then combine remaining ingredients in a jar; shake *or* mix well, and refrigerate. When ready to serve, pour dressing over salad. Toss lightly and serve.

Rose Ann's Tomato-Bean Salad

3 cloves garlic
1 tsp. oregano
1 Tbsp. olive oil
1 Tbsp. wine vinegar
2 cups halved cherry tomatoes
2 cups cooked green beans, chilled
lettuce

Mince garlic and mix with oregano, oil, and vinegar. Pour over tomatoes and beans; chill. Serve on a bed of lettuce. Serves 4 to 6. Stores well.

Sicilian Tomato Salad

1/4 cup white vinegar
1/2 cup water
1 Tbsp. dried parsley
1 Tbsp. dried basil
1 Tbsp. garlic pepper
    or
    1 tsp. garlic powder and
    1/4 tsp. fresh black pepper
1/2 tsp. sweetener
2 large tomatoes, cut in chunks

Mix all ingredients, except tomatoes. Place in deep bowl; add tomatoes and their juice. Toss lightly but thoroughly. Refrigerate one hour or more.

Vegetable Delight

1 small bunch broccoli, stems thinly
    sliced
1/2 head large cauliflower, separated
    into flowerets
3 carrots, cut into thin sticks
1 onion, sliced
2 Tbsp. salad oil
2 Tbsp. vinegar
2 Tbsp. prepared yellow mustard

In medium saucepan, place all vegetables in 1/2" lightly salted water and bring to boiling. Cover and simmer 3 minutes. Drain and refrigerate. Blend oil, vinegar, and mustard. Pour over vegetables and toss lightly. Refrigerate.

Variation: Add cherry tomatoes, radishes, and zucchini.

Zucchini Salad

2 zucchini, thinly sliced
2 tomatoes
1/2 green onion, chopped
1/4 small bell pepper, cut in strips
1 tsp. chopped parsley
2 tsp. vegetable oil
2 tsp. vinegar
1 small clove garlic, minced
1/4 tsp. salt
dash of pepper
2 tsp. water

Combine zucchini, tomatoes, green onion, bell pepper, and parsley in a bowl. In a jar, combine remaining ingredients; shake well. Pour over zucchini mixture. Chill several hours. Drain off marinade. Serve on lettuce leaves. Enough for 2.
Cheryl Doyle

Zucchini Toss-up

2 medium zucchini
1 Tbsp. lemon juice
garlic powder

1 medium green pepper, sliced
1 tsp. dried chives
2 medium tomatoes, quartered
2 Tbsp. wine vinegar
salt and pepper to taste
sweetener to equal 2 tsp. sugar
1 tsp. prepared mustard
1 tsp. oil, *optional*

Boil whole zucchini with lemon juice in just enough water to cover. Do not overcook. Drain. Slice zucchini into a wooden bowl; sprinkle with garlic powder. Add green pepper, chives, and tomatoes. Mix all other ingredients for dressing and pour over salad. Chill. Serves two.

POULTRY SALADS

Orange-Turkey Salad

1 orange, sawtooth cut in half, pulp removed
1/4 cup chopped orange pulp
2 Tbsp. orange juice
2 oz. cooked turkey, chopped
1/4 cup chopped celery
1/2 small tomato, cut in bite-sized pieces
salt to taste
pinch of parsley
1/2 cup chopped lettuce

Fill orange halves with all ingredients, except parsley and lettuce. Arrange on bed of chopped lettuce. Garnish with other half of the small tomato and parsley. Serves two.

Variation: For dinner portion, use 4 oz. cooked turkey.

Chicken and Fruit Salad

2 cups cubed, cooked chicken
1 cup halved seedless grapes
1 cup orange sections, fresh *or* canned
1 crisp green apple, diced
salt and pepper to taste
1/2 green pepper, diced
plain yogurt
parsley
1 Tbsp. sliced almonds *or* sunflower seeds

Mix first 6 ingredients together; moisten with yogurt. Place in serving bowl and chill. Garnish with parsley and nuts.

Fruity Chicken Salad

4 Tbsp. mayonnaise
2 Tbsp. skim milk
1 Tbsp. soy sauce
1/2 tsp. curry powder
1 Tbsp. lemon juice
1/4 tsp. salt
dash of pepper
16 oz. cooked chicken, cut up
1 cup chopped celery
2 wedges honeydew, cut into chunks *or* balls
1/2 cup pineapple chunks

Combine mayonnaise, milk, soy sauce, curry powder, lemon juice, salt, and pepper to make dressing. Mix with poultry, celery, melon, and pineapple. Chill. Serve over beds of lettuce.

Variations: Use turkey instead of chicken. Use cantaloupe instead of honeydew.

Chicken Salad Supreme

8 oz. chicken, cooked and cubed
1 medium apple, unpared and diced
lemon juice
1/2 cup finely diced celery
1/2 cup diced pimiento
1/2 cup diced green pepper
1/2 cup halved green or white grapes,
  seeded or seedless
mayonnaise
salt and pepper to taste
lettuce
parsley

Moisten apple with lemon juice. Set 4-5 grapes aside for garnish. Combine all ingredients, except lettuce and parsley, with enough mayonnaise to hold mixture together. Chill. Serve on lettuce bed garnished with remaining grapes and parsley.

Variations: Use sweet red pepper instead of pimiento. Use yogurt instead of mayonnaise.

FISH SALADS

Tuna and Vegetable Salad

2 large carrots, cut into 2" strips
1/2 small head cauliflower, broken in
  pieces
1/2 cup peas or green beans
1/2 cup thinly sliced celery
1/4 cup sliced green onion
1 6 1/2-oz. can water-packed tuna,
  drained

1/4 cup low-cal French dressing

Cook carrots and cauliflower together in small amount of boiling water for 10 minutes. Add peas or beans, and cook 5 minutes more until tender-crisp. Drain. In bowl, combine cooked vegetables, celery, onion, tuna, and dressing. Toss gently to coat, cover, and chill. Serve on lettuce leaf. Makes 3 servings at 224 calories per serving.

Stretch-A-Tuna Salad

1 1/2 cups crunchy rice or corn cereal
1 6 1/2-oz. can chunk, water-packed
  tuna, drained and flaked
2 hard-cooked eggs, finely chopped
1 apple, cored and chopped
1/2 cup chopped celery
1/2 cup pickle relish
2 tsp. finely chopped onion
1 tsp. lemon juice
2/3 cup yogurt, plain

Combine all ingredients. Stir lightly. Chill at least one hour. Serve on lettuce leaves. Makes 5-6 servings at about 140 calories per serving.

Sea Foam Salad

shredded lettuce or curly endive
8 oz. sole fillets, cooked, flaked,
  and chilled
2 pink grapefruits, pared and
  sectioned
1/2 cup chopped celery
1/4 cup low-cal French dressing

Place lettuce in a salad bowl. Arrange fish, grapefruit, and celery on top. Drizzle with dressing. Makes 4 servings.

MOLDED SALADS: *FRUIT-BASED*

Apple Salad

1 3/4 cups sugar-free red soda
2 envelopes unflavored gelatin
1/2 cup water
1/4 tsp. cinnamon
1 Tbsp. lemon juice
1 16-oz. can sugar-free applesauce
red food coloring
whole cloves
mint leaves, *optional*

Heat soda over low heat but do not boil. Sprinkle gelatin over water and allow to soften. Stir into soda with cinnamon, lemon juice, and applesauce. Add gelatin and stir until it dissolves. Add food coloring. Cool slightly; then pour into non-stick custard cups. Chill 4-6 hours. Unmold on lettuce leaves and insert clove in center of each salad. Garnish with 2-3 mint leaves, if desired to resemble apple stem and leaves. Serves 6-8.

Note: Use any red-colored soda.

Apple-Lime Salad

2 cups sugar-free applesauce
1 envelope dietetic lime gelatin
1 cup sugar-free lemon soda
12 small walnut halves

Combine applesauce and gelatin; cook until gelatin dissolves. Stir in soda and nuts. Pour into a mold; chill until firm, about 6 hours.

Happy Apple Mold

4 envelopes unflavored gelatin
2 1/2 cups boiling apple juice
sweetener to equal 4 Tbsp. sugar
12 walnuts, chopped

Dissolve gelatin in hot juice. Add other ingredients when gelatin is completely dissolved. Pour into a 2-qt. mold and refrigerate until firm.

Cheese Tropicale

2 envelopes dietetic lime gelatin
2 cups boiling water
1 can crushed pineapple
1 16-oz. carton cottage cheese

Dissolve gelatin thoroughly in hot water. Stir in pineapple and cottage cheese. Pour into a 1 1/2-qt. mold *or* bowl. Chill and serve.

Cherry Dream Salad

2 envelopes dietetic cherry gelatin
1 cup grape juice
1 cup cottage cheese
1 can crushed pineapple, drained

Dissolve gelatin in grape juice heated to boiling. Chill until firm. Whip and combine with cottage cheese and pineapple. Pour into a 1-qt. mold. Chill until firm.

Cranberry Delight

2 envelopes dietetic raspberry gelatin
1 cup chopped cranberries
1 cup chopped apple
1 cup drained, crushed pineapple
sweetener to equal 1 cup sugar

Prepare gelatin as directed on package. Add remaining ingredients. Pour into a 1-qt. mold or 8" square pan. Chill until firm.

Linda Rogers

Fruit Salad Delight

1/2 lb. cottage cheese
1 tangerine, sectioned
1 banana, peeled
1 apple, cored
1 envelope unflavored gelatin
sweetener to taste
allspice

Put all ingredients, except allspice, in blender, and process until smooth. Pour into a 2-qt. mold. Refrigerate until set. Garnish with extra fruit and allspice.

Grapefruit Salad

1 envelope unflavored gelatin
1/3 cup water
1 1/2 cups unsweetened grapefruit juice
1 cup pineapple chunks, drained
1 small can mandarin oranges, drained
1 small banana, sliced
sweetener

Dissolve gelatin in water. Boil grapefruit juice; add gelatin and cool until mixture begins to thicken. Add pineapple chunks, mandarin oranges, and banana slices. Add sweetener to taste. Pour into a 1-qt. mold. Refrigerate until firm.

Ginger Melon Salad

2 envelopes unflavored gelatin
1/2 cup cold water
1/2 cup lemon juice
sweetener to taste
2 cups sugar-free ginger ale
1/2 cup pineapple *or* melon

Sprinkle gelatin over cold water, heat, and dissolve. Add lemon juice, sweetener, and soda. Chill until thick. Add fruit and pour into a 1-qt. mold.

Heavenly Hash

2 envelopes dietetic gelatin, any flavor
1 16-oz. carton cottage cheese
1/2 cup drained, crushed pineapple
2 pkgs. low-cal whipped topping

Mix together dry gelatin and cottage cheese. Add pineapple. Whip topping as directed on package. Add to gelatin. Pour into a 2-qt. mold. Chill until set.

Note: Tint with red food coloring for the 4th of July; green for St. Patrick's Day, and pink for Easter.

Betty Lekan

Raspberry Surprise

2 envelopes dietetic raspberry gelatin
1 qt. frozen *or* canned raspberries

1 qt. buttermilk
1 cup boiling water

Dissolve gelatin in boiling water. Let chill until *slightly* thickened. Put raspberries and buttermilk in large bowl. Add gelatin and beat at low speed for 2 minutes. Put into a 6-cup mold or 13" x 9" x 2" pan. Refrigerate until firm.

Strawberry Cheese Supreme

1 1/3 cups cottage cheese
2/3 cup instant milk powder
3/4 cup sugar-free red soda
1 1/2 Tbsp. lemon juice
1/2 tsp. vanilla extract
1/2 tsp. strawberry extract
sweetener to equal 5 Tbsp. sugar
2 envelopes unflavored gelatin
2 cups sliced fresh strawberries

In blender, combine cottage cheese, milk powder, 1/2 cup red soda, lemon juice, vanilla, strawberry extract, and sweetener. Blend until smooth. Pour into large mixing bowl. In a saucepan sprinkle gelatin over 1/4 cup red soda; let soften. Stir over low heat until completely dissolved. Stir into cottage cheese mixture. Pour into gelatin mold; chill until set. Divide evenly. Makes 2 servings.

Tropical Upside-Down Salad

4 slices pineapple
3 maraschino cherries *or*
  3 strawberries
pineapple juice and water to equal
  1 1/2 cups
1 envelope dietetic orange gelatin
2/3 cups evaporated skim milk,
  undiluted
1 Tbsp. mayonnaise
6 walnuts, chopped

Cut each pineapple slice in 3 pieces, reserving liquid. Cut each cherry or strawberry in half. Put 2 pieces of pineapple and 1/2 a cherry or strawberry in bottom of 6 custard cups. Heat pineapple liquid and water to a boil. Add gelatin and stir to dissolve. Cool; add milk and mayonnaise. Blend. Add chopped nuts. Pour into molds. Chill. Unmold on lettuce.

Variation: Use as a dessert.

MOLDED SALADS: *FRUIT AND VEGETABLE COMBOS*

Holiday Salad

1 cup water
2 envelopes dietetic gelatin, any
  flavor
1 cup crushed pineapple, drained
1 cup evaporated skim milk
1/2 cup chopped celery
1 Tbsp. lemon juice
sweetener to taste

Dissolve gelatin in water and add remaining ingredients. Pour into a 1-qt. mold. Chill until firm.

Striped Vegetable Salad

1 envelope *each:* dietetic raspberry, lemon, and pineapple gelatin
1 cup crushed pineapple
1 Tbsp. lemon juice
1/2 cup finely grated carrot
1 dill pickle, finely chopped
1 cup finely chopped celery

Prepare raspberry gelatin per directions and chill until slightly thickened. Fold pineapple into gelatin. Pour into a 9" x 5" loaf pan; chill until firm. Prepare lemon gelatin; fold in carrots and pour over red layer. Chill until firm. Prepare lime gelatin; fold in dill pickle and celery. Pour over lemon layer. Chill. Unmold when firm.

Seedless Grape and Asparagus Aspic

2 cups canned asparagus tips, drained
3 Tbsp. reserved asparagus liquid
1 Tbsp. or 1 envelope unflavored gelatin
chicken stock
dash of paprika
2 cups seedless grapes
1 cup chopped celery
yogurt

Soak gelatin in asparagus liquid. Heat remaining liquid and dissolve gelatin in it. Add chicken stock to make a total of 2 cups liquid. Season with paprika and chill. When nearly set, combine with grapes, celery, and asparagus tips. Pour into a 1 1/2-qt. mold. Chill until firm. Unmold and serve with yogurt.

Waldorf Salad

1 envelope unflavored gelatin
1 tsp. sweetener
1/2 tsp. salt
1 1/2 cups water
1/4 cup lemon juice
2 cups diced apples
1/2 cup diced celery
1/4 cup crushed pineapple

Mix gelatin, sweetener, salt, and 1/4 cup water. Place over low heat, stirring until gelatin is dissolved. Remove from heat and stir in remaining water and lemon juice. Chill to consistency of unbeaten egg white. Fold in diced apples, celery, and pineapple. Pour into a 4-cup mold and chill until firm.

MOLDED SALADS: *VEGETABLE-BASED*

Cucumber Mold

1 envelope unflavored gelatin
1/2 cup cold water
1 tsp. parsley flakes
1 tsp. salt
2 Tbsp. lemon juice
dash of cayenne pepper
1 1/2 cups chicken bouillon
1 stalk celery, cut in pieces
1 cup coarsely grated cucumber
1 tsp. snipped fresh dill
1/2 cup thinly sliced radishes

Sprinkle gelatin over water to soften; set aside. Combine parsley, salt, lemon juice, pepper, bouillon, and celery in a saucepan. Simmer 20 minutes and strain. Add softened gelatin to hot broth, and stir until gelatin dissolves. Chill until mixture mounds slightly when dropped from spoon. Add cucumber, dill, and radishes. Turn into a 3-cup mold. Chill until firm.

Perfection Salad

1 envelope unflavored gelatin
1 1/2 cups water
1 tsp. liquid sweetener
1 Tbsp. lemon juice
1/4 tsp. salt
1/2 cup shredded cabbage
1/2 cup shredded carrot
1/4 cup finely chopped green pepper

Soften gelatin in 1/2 cup cold water; dissolve in 1 cup boiling water. Stir in sweetener, lemon juice, and salt. Chill until thick but not set. Fold in vegetables. Pour into a 7" x 3" loaf pan. Chill until firm.

MOLDED SALADS: FISH-BASED

Salmon Salad

12 oz. sugar-free orange soda
2 envelopes unflavored gelatin
2 Tbsp. lemon juice
1 stalk celery, diced
1/2 green pepper, diced
1/2 cucumber, thinly sliced
1 can red salmon, drained and
  chopped

Dissolve gelatin in 1/2 cup soda. Heat remaining soda to a boil; add gelatin and lemon juice. Cool to room temperature. Add celery, pepper, cucumber, and salmon. Pour into a 1-qt. mold. Refrigerate.

MOLDED SALADS: POULTRY-BASED

Molded Turkey Salad

2 envelopes unflavored gelatin
1/2 cup cold water
3 chicken bouillon cubes
3 cups boiling water
3 Tbsp. lemon juice
3 Tbsp. horseradish
2 Tbsp. onion flakes
12 oz. cooked turkey
3/4 cup diced celery
1 medium green pepper, chopped

Sprinkle gelatin over cold water to soften. Let stand 5 minutes. In a bowl, combine bouillon cubes and boiling water; stir until cubes dissolve. Add softened gelatin; stir to dissolve. Add lemon juice, horseradish, and onion flakes. Refrigerate until mixture mounds when dropped from spoon. Fold in turkey, celery, and green pepper. Spoon into a 9" x 5" loaf pan or a 2-qt. mold. Refrigerate until firm. Unmold onto plate and garnish as desired.

Nancy Walters

Molded Pineapple Chicken Salad

1 envelope dietetic lemon gelatin
1/2 tsp. salt, *optional*
2 cups boiling chicken broth
1 2/3 cups finely diced cooked chicken
1 8 1/2-oz. can crushed pineapple, drained
1/4 cup halved white grapes
2 Tbsp. minced onion
2 Tbsp. chopped pimiento

Dissolve gelatin and salt in boiling broth. Chill until thick. Fold in remaining ingredients and pour into a 4-cup mold. Chill until firm. Unmold. Serve on lettuce.

SALAD DRESSINGS

French Dressing Supreme

sweetener to equal 1/2 cup sugar
1/8 tsp. salt
2 tsp. paprika
1 cup tomato juice
1/2 cup vinegar
1/8 tsp. dry mustard
2 Tbsp. celery seed
1 Tbsp. onion flakes

Combine all ingredients, blend well, and refrigerate.

Make up small amounts of special dressings, using the variations below with your basic recipes. Combine in mini-containers in your blender. Suit the basic dressing recipe to the type of salad:

a cottage-cheese blend for coleslaw
a garlicky taste for mixed greens
lemon juice for tangy freshness
packet low-cal blue cheese for flavor
2 Tbsp. herbs for flavor
orange juice, blended citrus fruit, brown sugar sweetener *or* yogurt for fruit salad

Mock Sour Cream

1 Tbsp. lemon juice
1 *or* 2 Tbsp. skim milk
1/2 cup cottage cheese
pinch of salt

Place lemon juice and skim milk in blender. Gradually add cottage cheese and salt, blending at low speed. Blend a few minutes at high speed until smooth. Thin mixture if necessary with remaining skim milk. Use on vegetables or use to stuff celery.

Cheryl Doyle

Mayonnaise Supreme

4 tsp. liquid sweetener
1 tsp. dry mustard
1/2 cup cider vinegar
1 tsp. cold water
2 cups buttermilk
2 tsp. salt
1/4 tsp. black pepper
1 pkg. unflavored gelatin
1 Tbsp. onion flakes, *optional*

Place sweetener, mustard, pepper, vinegar, and salt in feeder cap of blender. Add dissolved gelatin, buttermilk, salt, and onion flakes. Process at BLEND. If necessary, stop blender, and use spatula to keep mixture around processing blades. Replace feeder cap and continue to process until well blended. Remove through bottom opening and refrigerate until set. Remove from refrigerator and blend until smooth. Return to refrigerator.

Rose Ann's Quick Mayonnaise

1 cup plain yogurt
1 raw egg yolk
2 Tbsp. lemon juice

Mix all ingredients together and chill at least two hours. Use it as a milk, instead of a fat, exchange.

Orange Blossom Dressing

1 can evaporated skim milk
1 can frozen orange juice
   concentrate, thawed

In jar, shake above ingredients until mixed. Good over fruit and only 20 calories per tablespoon.

Pimiento Dressing

1 7 1/2 or 8 oz. jar pimiento
4 mild cherry peppers
1/4 cup vinegar
1 Tbsp. lemon juice
1 Tbsp. soy sauce
sweetener to equal 1/3 cup sugar or
   to taste

Combine all ingredients and blend. If chunky dressing is preferred, additional chopped pimiento can be added after blending.

Judy Booster

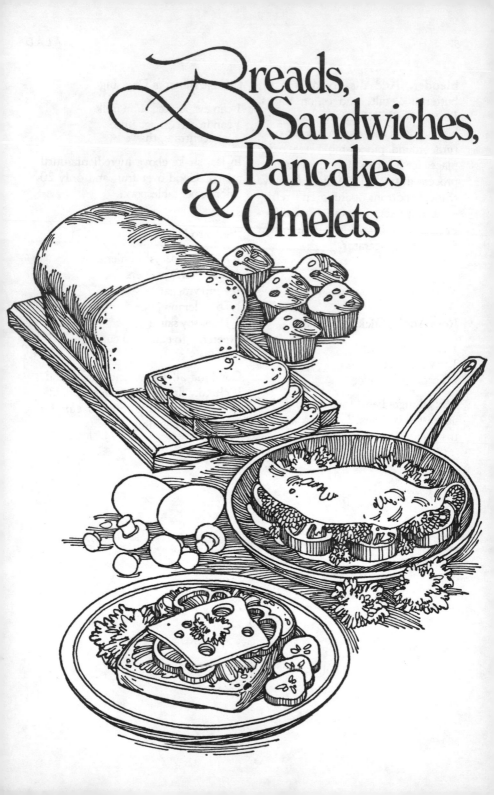

Breads, Sandwiches, Pancakes & Omelets

When you're in a hurry, it's easy to reach for fattening foods. Slow down and try these low-calorie recipes.

Pocket bread filled with a simple vegetable or sprout filling can make a hearty and slimming noon meal. Double or triple the recipe and you'll have plenty to freeze!

Pancakes make tasty light lunch and supper candidates. Be creative and open to varying your meals. Try an omelet for dinner!

Breads in careful measure need not be your downfall.

Comfort thine heart with a morsel of bread, and afterwards go thine way . . .

is a bit of sound advice from Judges 19:5 (KJV). Enjoy your starches in morsel amounts and then be on your busy way!

POINTERS TO HEALTHFUL EATING

Bread averages 80 calories per slice or per 1/2 bun. Don't be mislead into thinking you can indulge in any amount of bread and not suffer for it! Thinly sliced wheat bread is a nutritionally good choice. We suggest women and teens have 1 ounce of bread for breakfast and 1 ounce for lunch. Men may have double that amount.

Be careful with the fillings. If the filling is protein, then add vegetables to stretch out the protein mixture or reduce the protein amount to half.

Avoid large amounts of mayonnaise or cheese. A pleasant addition is the use of yogurt as a spread. Try 1/3 mayonnaise and 2/3 yogurt. Another tangy addition is mustard which goes well with many types of filling.

Add seeds and nuts sparingly. Six nuts or one tablespoon of seeds is equal to one fat portion or about 45 calories!

BREADS

Homemade Pocket Bread

3 1/2 to 4 cups flour
1 pkg. active dry yeast
2 Tbsp. cooking oil
1 tsp. salt
1/4 tsp. sugar
1/2 cup warm water

In electric mixer, blend 1 1/2 cups flour and remaining ingredients. Beat on low speed for 30 seconds, scraping sides of bowl often. Stir in enough remaining flour to make a moderately stiff dough. Turn dough out onto a lightly floured surface; knead about 5 minutes until smooth and elastic. Cover; let rise 45 minutes. Punch down and divide into 12 equal pieces. Shape into balls, cover, and let rest 10 minutes. Roll each ball out onto a lightly floured surface to a 5" circle. *Do not roll back and forth or bread will not puff.*

Place dough 2" apart on ungreased baking sheet. Cover and let rise 20-30 minutes. Bake at 400° for 10-20 minutes until puffed and brown. To serve, slice halfway down one side and stuff with sandwich filling of choice. Makes 12 pockets, each equal to 1 bread portion.

Banana Nut Bread #1

1/2 tsp. baking soda
1 capful butter flavoring
2 eggs
10 tsp. sweetener
4 Tbsp. water
2 tsp. walnut extract
2 tsp. vanilla
2 medium bananas, mashed
2/3 cup instant milk powder
6 Tbsp. hominy grits

Beat together all ingredients except milk powder and grits. Slowly add dry milk and grits. Mix well and bake in a small loaf pan at 350° for 25 minutes or until golden brown.
D. J. Davis

Banana Nut Bread #2

2 eggs, well beaten
1 small banana, mashed
1/2 cup drained, crushed pineapple
1 small apple, grated
1/4 tsp. baking soda
1/4 tsp. salt
1/4 tsp. butter flavoring
1 to 1 1/2 tsp. liquid sweetener
1 tsp. vanilla
6 Tbsp. oatmeal or quick grits
2/3 cup instant milk powder

Mix all ingredients together and pour into a small, non-stick loaf pan. Bake at 350° for 35-40 minutes.
Katie Blimke

Pumpkin Bread

2 eggs, well beaten
1/2 cup cooked pumpkin
1/3 cup instant milk powder
1/2 tsp. cinnamon
1/2 tsp. nutmeg
1/2 tsp. ginger
1/2 tsp. salt

1/4 tsp. baking soda
1 tsp. liquid sweetener
1 cup dry oatmeal
1 Tbsp. chopped nuts
2 Tbsp. raisins

Mix all ingredients, except last three. Then add oatmeal, beating well. Stir in nuts and raisins. Pour into a small, non-stick loaf pan. Bake at 350° for 40-45 minutes.

Bernie Deprez

Garlic Biscuits

tube of five ready-made biscuits
garlic powder

Sprinkle the top of biscuits with garlic powder. Bake as directed. Butter lightly to eat.

Note: One biscuit is equivalent to a slice of bread.

Blueberry Muffins

2 slices bread
2 egg yolks
1/4 tsp. butter flavoring
1 tsp. almond extract
1/3 cup instant milk powder
3 Tbsp. water
2 1/2 tsp. sweetener
2 egg whites
1/2 cup blueberries

Blend bread in blender; place in a bowl. Add egg yolks and mix well. Add flavorings, milk, water, and sweetener. Beat egg whites to form a peak. Gently fold into batter. Add blueberries. Pour into a 6-cup muffin tin. Bake at 350° for 20-25 minutes.

Fruit Muffins

1/2 cup applesauce
1 cup frozen berries of choice
2/3 cup milk powder
2 eggs
3 Tbsp. cornmeal
3 Tbsp. oatmeal
sweetener to taste
1 Tbsp. walnut extract
1 Tbsp. butter flavoring
1/4 tsp. baking powder
1/4 tsp. salt

Mix all ingredients together. Bake in muffin tins at 350° for 20 minutes.

Danish Pastry

Dough:
2 eggs
2 slices bread
1 tsp. baking powder
2/3 cup instant milk powder
2 pkgs. *or* 4 tsp. sweetener
1/2 tsp. orange extract
1 tsp. butter flavoring

Cheese Topping:
8 oz. ricotta cheese
1/2 cup non-sugared crunchy cereal
1/4 tsp. almond extract
3 pkgs. *or* 6 tsp. sweetener

Mix all ingredients for dough together. Beat well. Pour into nonstick miniature muffin tins. Mix together all ingredients for *Cheese Topping*. Divide mixture evenly over tops. Bake at 350° for 20 minutes. Makes 16 miniatures.

SANDWICHES

Asparagus Cheese

1 slice white toast
1 thin slice tomato
3 spears asparagus
1 oz. slice Swiss cheese
dash of paprika

Top toast with remaining ingredients. Place under broiler until heated through. Serve with parsley and dill pickle, if desired.

Open-Faced Chicken and Pepper

1 English muffin *or* hard roll
1/4 cup orange juice
4 oz. finely chopped chicken
1/2 green pepper
1/4 cup canned mushrooms, drained
dash of onion flakes
1/2 tomato, chopped
sweetener
nutmeg
1 tsp. cornstarch

Halve muffin or roll; set aside. Heat remaining ingredients together and season slightly with sweetener and nutmeg. Thicken sauce with cornstarch. Spoon over bread halves and toast under broiler.

Chicken and Pineapple Sandwich

3 oz. cubed chicken
1/2 cup crushed pineapple
1/2 Tbsp. mayonnaise
1 Tbsp. chopped green pepper
salt and pepper to taste

Mix all ingredients together and spread on bread. Leave open-faced and cut into triangles.

Czar Sandwich

1 slice rye bread
1 slice hard-cooked egg
1 cooked, crumbled bacon strip *or*
  2 tsp. bacon bits
2 Tbsp. chopped mushrooms
2 Tbsp. low-cal Russian dressing
1/2 oz. grated cheese

Top bread with remaining ingredients. Broil until cheese melts.

Egg Salad

2 eggs, hard-cooked and quartered
low-cal mayonnaise *or* plain yogurt
1 tsp. mustard
thin bread
lettuce

Place eggs in blender, cover, and process at STIR 1 cycle. Combine with mayonnaise and mustard for a sandwich spread. Serve on bread with lettuce.

Healthwich

1 slice toast
2 thin slices avocado
1 Tbsp. chopped green pepper
2 thin slices tomato
2 large Tbsp. alfalfa sprouts
1/2 slice Muenster cheese

Top toast with remaining ingredients. Broil until melted.

Petite Pizzas

toasted English muffin halves
2 Tbsp. tomato juice
dash of garlic powder
dash of oregano
1/2 oz. grated Muenster cheese

Optional garnishes:
mushrooms
onions
green peppers
or other vegetables

Spread halves with juice-cheese mixture. Broil until cheese is melted. Garnish with vegetables, if desired.

Note: 1/2 English muffin is equivalent to 1 slice of bread.

Pita Rarebit

1/2 pita bread
1/2 chopped egg
chopped cabbage
green pepper
mushrooms
1 oz. grated cheese

Stuff bread with egg and vegetables. Top with cheese. Broil until cheese is melted.

Reuben Special

1 slice toast
1 Tbsp. prepared mustard
2 heaping Tbsp. sauerkraut
caraway seeds
1/2 slice Swiss cheese

Spread toast with remaining ingredients. Melt under broiler.

Seafood Delight

1 English muffin, bagel, *or* hard roll, halved
1 oz. water-packed tuna
1 Tbsp. plain yogurt
1 Tbsp. chopped green pepper
onion flakes
2 Tbsp. chopped celery
1 Tbsp. chopped dill pickle
1 oz. Muenster cheese

Top bread with all ingredients, adding cheese last. Toast under broiler until cheese melts.

Broiled Tuna Cheese

1 slice rye bread
1 1/2 oz. tuna fish
1/2 oz. Muenster cheese

Place tuna fish on rye bread and top with cheese. Broil until cheese melts.

Helen Reed

Tuna Cover-Up

3/4 cups tomato juice
1/2 green pepper, diced
1 stalk Chinese cabbage, diced
1 Tbsp. parsley flakes
celery salt
garlic salt
1 7-oz. can tuna, drained and flaked
1/2 can mushrooms

Cook first 6 ingredients until juice thickens. Place tuna on 1 slice of toast; cover with sauce. Garnish with mushrooms.

Sweet Sprout Delight

rye bread
several slices green pepper
fresh alfalfa sprouts
1 thin slice tomato
1 oz. slice Swiss cheese
1 Tbsp. raisins
1 walnut half

Spread bread with remaining ingredients, ending with raisins and walnut half. Broil until melted.

SANDWICH SPREADS

Guacamole Egg Spread

1/2 avocado, mashed
1 Tbsp. chopped pimiento
2 hard-cooked eggs, chopped
1 Tbsp. lime or lemon juice
1/4 tsp. hot sauce
1/4 cup chopped dill pickles

Mix ingredients together. This yields about 1 1/4 cups.

Nature Sandwich Spread

1/2 cup plain yogurt
1/4 cup cottage cheese
1/2 cup shredded yellow cheese
1/4 cup wheat germ
12 walnut meats, chopped
1 Tbsp. bacon-bits
1 Tbsp. chopped onion

Mix ingredients together and chill. Makes about 1 1/2 cups spread.

Peanut Butter-Slaw Spread

4 Tbsp. peanut butter
2 Tbsp. sugar-free applesauce
1/2 tsp. curry powder
1/3 cup grated carrot
1/3 cup chopped green pepper
1/3 cup finely shredded cabbage

Mix ingredients together. This yields about 1 cup.

Tuna-Orange Spread

1 7-oz. can water-packed tuna, drained and flaked
1 tsp. grated orange peel
1 orange, peeled and diced
6 walnut halves, chopped
4 Tbsp. plain yogurt

Mix ingredients together. This yields about 2 cups.

PANCAKES

Berry Pancakes

1 slice white bread
1 egg
6-8 drops liquid sweetener, optional
cinnamon
1/2 cup fresh or frozen berries
orange slices

Process first 3 ingredients in blender until smooth. Pour into pancake-sized circles in a non-stick pan. Brown until set and turn. Place on plate and sprinkle with cinnamon. Garnish with fresh berries and an orange slice. Serves one person.

Note: Recipe makes fine crepes.

Holiday Berry Pancakes

1 slice white bread
1 egg
6 drops sweetener
1/2 cup liquid skim milk
1/2 cup berries, fresh or frozen
1 tsp. margarine
cinnamon

Mix first 5 ingredients in blender. Using margarine on a non-stick pan, pour batter as silver-dollar pancakes. Sprinkle with cinnamon and garnish with a fresh berry, if desired.

Zucchini Pancakes

2 cups grated zucchini (drain, if too watery)
2 Tbsp. grated onion
2 eggs, slightly beaten
6 Tbsp. flour
dash of butter-salt or liquid butter flavoring

Mix all ingredients together, dropping by teaspoonful onto a non-stick pan. Make silver-dollar size and cook as a pancake. Top with low-calorie syrup.

Mary Lou Rachwal

OMELETS

Basic Omelet

3 eggs
2 Tbsp. water
salt and pepper to taste
1 tsp. margarine
Filling

Beat eggs, water, salt, and pepper until blended but not frothy. In an 8" skillet, melt margarine and coat pan. Pour in egg mixture and cook over medium heat; using a fork, rapidly stir in a zigzag pattern just through top of uncooked eggs. Shake skillet constantly to keep the egg mixture moving. When eggs are set, remove from heat. Add *Filling*.

Filling:
lemon juice to taste
dash of tarragon
salt and pepper to taste
desired vegetables

In small pan, stir ingredients together. When still warm, place in middle of omelet and fold over.

Variation: Add 1 oz. grated cheese on top and let melt in oven or microwave.

Fruit 'N Cheese Omelet

1 *Basic Omelet*
Filling:
3 Tbsp. orange juice
sweetener to equal 2 Tbsp. sugar
1 tsp. lemon juice
1 tsp. cornstarch
3/4 cup mixed fruit
1/4 cup shredded Muenster cheese

For filling, combine all ingredients except fruit and cheese. Cook and stir until thick and bubbly. Stir in fruit and heat through. Fold into omelet. Top with shredded cheese.

Egg Foo Yung

4 eggs
1 Tbsp. milk
1/2 tsp. salt
1 can water chestnuts, drained
1/2 small onion
1 can bean sprouts, drained
1 4 1/2-oz. can shrimp, drained
1 Tbsp. water

Put all ingredients, except shrimp and water, in blender. Blend well. Stir in shrimp. Heat water in fry pan. Measure 1/4 cup per patty, and pour egg mixture onto pre-heated surface. When browned, turn. Place on warm serving platter. Serve with *sauce*. Makes about 10 patties 60 calories each.

Sauce:
3/4 cup water
1 Tbsp. cornstarch
2 Tbsp. soy sauce
sweetener to equal 1 Tbsp. sugar
1 Tbsp. cider vinegar

Combine all ingredients in a saucepan. Heat on medium heat until clear and slightly thick.

Variation: Leftover pork, chicken, or tuna may be used instead of shrimp.

Eggs Jambalaya

1 small onion
3 stalks celery
4 tsp. tomato juice
1 can mushrooms, drained
1 can chop suey vegetables, drained
2 Tbsp. soy sauce

dash of garlic powder
4 eggs

Sauté all ingredients, except eggs. Beat in eggs; heat mixture and stir until eggs are set. Makes 2-3 large portions.

Low-Cholesterol Western Omelet

1 container egg substitute
1/2 cup chopped green pepper
2 Tbsp. minced onion
1 oz. chopped turkey ham
dash of pepper
1 tsp. margarine

Melt margarine in 10" pan over medium-low heat. Combine egg substitute and remaining ingredients. Pour into pan and cook about 10 minutes until set. Cut into wedges. Serve each on a slice of whole wheat toast. Makes 4 servings.

Simple Supper Omelet

1 onion, sliced
1 Tbsp. water
salt and pepper to taste
1/2 green pepper, diced
1 can mushrooms, drained and chopped
1/2 cup fresh mung bean sprouts
6 Tbsp. skim milk
1 tsp. soy sauce
1 Tbsp. chopped dried parsley
4 eggs
2 tomatoes, sliced

Sauté onions in water until soft. Add salt, pepper, green pepper, chopped mushrooms, and sprouts.

Cover and cook 4-5 minutes until tender and heated. Beat eggs and add milk, soy sauce, and parsley; pour into pan with cooked vegetables. Cover and steam, stirring once or twice. When almost set, add tomatoes and heat through. Makes 2 servings.

Vegetable Dishes

FIVE

"You sit right there until you finish your vegetables!" Do you recall your mother saying that to you as a youngster? Have you perhaps said that to your own children? Keep up this negative approach and you'll predispose your children to becoming vegetable-hating adults!

A nutrition journal suggests we tell them instead, "Eat your ice cream or you can't have any broccoli." This approach makes vegetables sound more appealing and special—and rightly so!

Time, energy, and thought. What do you do with these ingredients of food planning? If serving vegetables to your family brings more *ughs* than approval, now's the time to make a new turn for the better. Raw, steamed, or braised vegetables deserve a place of honor on your table.

Try two new recipes each week from this section, and see if a new attitude toward vegetables doesn't set in after all. In fact,

... *forget all that* [the past]—*it is nothing compared to what I'm going to do! For I'm going to do a brand new thing. See, I have already begun! Don't you see it?*

Isaiah 43:18, 19 (TLB)

POINTERS TO HEALTHFUL EATING

High in fiber, vitamins, and minerals, most vegetables are indispensable for weight control. That means eat as much of them as you want, in general!

Keep in mind that Group A vegetables are low in natural sugar content; one cup of these contains around 25 calories. One cup of Group B vegetables has about 80 calories, so be alert!

Take into account recipes with cheese protein. An occasional recipe might also include a bread portion which you should count as part of your daily total. Amnesia eating—leaving out some items in the daily total—still shows up in a pound weight!

ASPARAGUS

Asparagus Bake

1 can asparagus, saving juice
1 egg
1 slice bread, toasted
paprika
parsley

Put asparagus in small baking dish. Blend egg, bread, and juice of asparagus in the blender. Pour over baking dish ingredients and sprinkle with paprika and parsley flakes. Bake at 350° until egg is done, about 5-10 minutes.

BROCCOLI

Broccoli with Orange Sauce

1/2 cup orange juice
dash of nutmeg
1 Tbsp. grated orange rind
1/2 Tbsp. arrowroot
1 pkg. broccoli spears, cooked and drained

Place orange juice, nutmeg, and grated orange rind in a saucepan, and heat. Thicken with arrowroot. Serve over broccoli.

Creamed Broccoli and Onions

2 10-oz. pkgs. frozen *or* 1 1/2 lbs. fresh broccoli
1/2 cup diced onion
2/3 cup yogurt
1 tsp. garlic powder

1 tsp. salt
dash of pepper

Cook broccoli until tender. Add onions during last two minutes. Combine remaining ingredients in a bowl. Drain vegetables well and combine with bowl ingredients. Serves 6.

Rose Ann's Broccoli Crisp

2 10-oz. pkgs. frozen chopped broccoli
1 1/2 cups chopped onion
1 2-oz. jar pimiento, chopped
2/3 cup plain yogurt
1 tsp. garlic
1 tsp. parsley
1/4 tsp. pepper
1 pt. cherry tomatoes

Defrost broccoli on paper towel. After all moisture is absorbed, mix well with onion and pimiento. Add remaining ingredients and stir gently. Cover and chill at least 3 hours. Keeps well for 2 days. Serves 8-10. Serve on a salad plate lined with a lettuce or spinach leaf.

Variation: Add diced celery to mixture.

CABBAGE

Scalloped Cabbage

1 head cabbage, cut into small pieces
2 cups milk
1 Tbsp. arrowroot
1/2 tsp. butter flavoring

2 Tbsp. onion flakes
parsley

Combine all ingredients and put into a Pam-sprayed casserole dish. Bake at 350° for 1 hour.

Scrambled Cabbage

1 Tbsp. margarine
3 cups finely shredded cabbage
1 cup thinly sliced celery
1 medium onion, sliced thinly
1/2 medium green pepper, chopped
2 tomatoes, peeled and chopped
sweetener to taste
1 tsp. salt
1/4 tsp. pepper

Melt margarine in skillet. Stir in vegetables. Add sweetener, salt, and pepper. Cover and cook over medium heat 5 minutes or until vegetables are tender-crisp. Stir occasionally.

Snappy Orange Cabbage

1 1/4 lbs. or 1 small head red
    cabbage, thinly sliced
1/4 cup frozen orange juice
    concentrate, thawed
1 1/2 tsp. salt
dash of pepper

In a large saucepan, cook cabbage in boiling water about 3 minutes; drain. Stir orange juice, salt, and pepper together. Add cabbage; cover and simmer 20 minutes.

Variation: Add cornstarch and water to cabbage; stir until smooth.

CARROTS

Carrot Pudding

1 lb. carrots, peeled and quartered
2 Tbsp. skim milk
1 egg
1/2 tsp. salt
sweetener to equal 1 Tbsp. sugar
dash of cloves
dash of pepper
1 Tbsp. margarine
1/3 cup finely chopped onion
2 Tbsp. chopped parsley

Cook carrots until tender; drain. Beat with electric mixer until smooth. Blend in milk, egg, salt, sweetener, cloves, and pepper. Melt margarine; add onion and parsley, cooking until tender. Stir into carrot mixture. Turn into a non-stick casserole and bake at 350° for 30 minutes or until set. Serves 4 at 50 calories per serving.

Note: Can use microwave on high for 12 minutes.

Maple-Glazed Carrots

1-lb. can carrots, drained
2 Tbsp. sugar-free maple syrup
1 tsp. butter-salt

Combine all ingredients in saucepan. Cover pan and simmer mixture over low heat for 10 minutes, stirring occasionally. Serves 4.

Saucy Cheddar Carrots

1/2 cup chopped onion
2 stalks celery, diced
1 tsp. margarine
1/2 tsp. dry mustard
dash of pepper
2/3 cup instant milk powder
1/4 cup water
1 lb. carrots, cooked and cut into
  strips
2 oz. Cheddar cheese, shredded

Stove-Top Method:
Sauté onion and celery in margarine until tender. Stir in remaining ingredients, except cheese; cook over medium heat, stirring well. Add cheese during the last two minutes. Serves 6.

Microwave Method:
In a 1-qt. glass dish, simmer onion, celery, and margarine on high for 2 minutes. Stir in all other ingredients. Cover with wax paper and cook 5 minutes until hot, giving dish a turn every 2 minutes. Stir and serve.

CARROTS: *CARROT WINNERS*

Skillet Carrots
2 tsp. diet margarine
4 medium carrots, coarsely shredded
salt
parsley

Melt margarine in skillet. Add carrots. Sprinkle with salt. Cover and cook just until tender, about 5-8 minutes. Top with snipped parsley. Serves 2.

...d Carrots
...p granulated sweetener

2 Tbsp. diet margarine
1/2 tsp. cinnamon
4 cooked carrots, whole or halved
  lengthwise

Heat together sweetener and margarine until sugar dissolves. Add cinnamon. Mix well. Add carrots. Cook over medium heat, turning carrots until well glazed and tender, about 12 minutes. Serves 2.

Basil Carrots
2 Tbsp. diet margarine
6 medium carrots, thinly sliced
  on bias
1/4 tsp. salt
1/4 tsp. dried basil, crushed

In medium skillet, melt margarine. Add carrots. Sprinkle with salt and basil. Cover; simmer 10-12 minutes or until tender. Serves 6.

Cheryl Doyle

CAULIFLOWER

Aromatic Cauliflower

5 cups chicken bouillon
2 cups chopped cauliflower
1/4 cup uncooked brown rice
1 small onion, minced
1 small carrot, thinly sliced
1/4 cup chopped celery
2/3 cup fresh *or* frozen peas
1/4 tsp. onion salt
salt and pepper
1/8 tsp. dry mustard
1 cup skim milk *or* 1 cup evaporated
  skim milk
2 oz. Muenster cheese *or* grated
  Romano cheese

In a large pot, heat bouillon to boiling. Add remaining ingredients, except milk and cheese. Cover and simmer over low heat until vegetables are tender. Add milk and cheese. Stir constantly until cheese is melted. Makes 8 cups.

Cream of Cauliflower in Squash

1 acorn squash, halved and seeded
1 pkg. frozen cauliflower
2 chicken bouillon cubes
2 cups water
1 Tbsp. dehydrated onion flakes
1 tsp. chives
1 cup skim milk
1 cup buttermilk
1 tsp. butter flavoring
salt and pepper to taste

Bake acorn squash cut side down in a shallow baking dish at 350° for 35-40 minutes. Turn cut side up, salt, and bake an additional 20 minutes. Meanwhile, combine next 5 ingredients and simmer until tender. Either chop or mash cauliflower; then add skim milk, buttermilk, flavoring, salt, and pepper. Simmer until heated. Serve in hot acorn squash halves.

CUCUMBERS

Stuffed Cucumbers

1 cucumber, cut in half lengthwise
4 oz. cottage cheese
1 tsp. onion salt
1 green pepper, chopped

1 tsp. pimiento
1 tsp. celery seed
dash of garlic powder
1 Tbsp. diced celery
2 Tbsp. French dressing

Hollow out cucumber halves. Mix remaining ingredients together and stuff into cucumber hollows. Garnish as desired.

Gazpacho

2 green onions, diced
1 medium tomato, diced
1/2 cup diced cucumber
1/4 cup diced green pepper
1/4 cup chopped mushrooms
1/4 cup red wine vinegar

Combine all ingredients and chill.

GREEN BEANS

Italian Beans

1/4 cup dietetic Italian dressing
1 9-oz. can French-style green beans, partially thawed
1 onion, chopped
pimiento
2 tsp. dill

Place beans, salad dressing, pimiento, and onion in small skillet. Cook until beans are thawed, separating with a fork as they cook. Do not overcook. Add dill and continue cooking just until beans and onions are tender-crisp.

Lemony Green Beans

1/2 lb. green beans, trimmed and
  cut in 1" lengths
1 tsp. melted margarine
pinch of salt
dash of pepper
1 Tbsp. minced parsley
juice of 1/2 lemon

Cook beans in a small amount of
salted water until they are tender-
crisp. Drain and put in a serving
dish. Mix remaining ingredients, and
pour over green beans. Serve hot.

Cheryl Doyle

Savory Green Beans

1 lb. green beans, cut into 3" lengths
1/4 lb. fresh mushrooms, sliced
1 Tbsp. margarine
2 Tbsp. sliced green onion
1/2 cup water
2 Tbsp. snipped *or* dried parsley
dash of sweetener
dash of hot pepper sauce
1 Tbsp. vinegar
1 Tbsp. lemon juice
1 tsp. dried savory leaves
1/2 tsp. salt

Set beans aside. Place mushrooms,
margarine, and onions in a 2-qt.
casserole. Cook 2-4 minutes on high,
stirring once. Set aside. Place beans
in saucepan; add water to cover.
Cook on high for about 15 minutes,
stirring every 5 minutes until beans
are tender; add onion mixture and
other seasonings. Toss to mix. Cover
and cook 3 minutes longer, stirring
once. Serves 4.

MUSHROOMS

Duxelles

1/2 lb. whole mushrooms, chopped
1/4 cup chopped onions, *or* 2 Tbsp.
  shallots
2 tsp. margarine
salt and pepper to taste
dash of nutmeg

Sauté all ingredients on high heat
until moisture is absorbed. Store in
covered jar in refrigerator.

Variation: Use stems instead of whole
mushrooms. Use as flavoring for
meats and vegetables or as a stuffing
for turkey or mushrooms.

Lemony Mushrooms

2 Tbsp. lemon juice
1/8 tsp. salt
1/4 tsp. pepper
1 lb. fresh mushrooms, cleaned

Sauté all ingredients in uncovered
frying pan until lightly browned. Stir
occasionally.

Mushroom Ecstasy

1/2 lb. mushrooms
1 green pepper, sliced as desired
1/4 medium onion, sliced as desired
garlic powder to taste
salt and pepper to taste

In a Pam-sprayed pan, sauté onion
and green pepper at medium-low
heat. Meanwhile, wash and soak
fresh mushrooms in cold water for
3-4 minutes. Slice or quarter mush-

rooms into pan with onion and pepper. Sprinkle garlic, salt, and pepper over mixture. Cook several minutes. Serve.

Note: This mixture is ideal on hamburger *or* steak.

Vicki Garrett

Stuffed Mushrooms

1 lb. large mushrooms, cleaned
5 Tbsp. dehydrated *or* fresh onions
5 Tbsp. minced celery
bouillon
water
5 Tbsp. bread crumbs
Parmesan cheese

Remove mushroom stems; mince with onion and celery. Sauté in heavy skillet with a sprinkle of any flavor bouillon and water to keep vegetables from sticking—without adding fat and calories. Add bread crumbs and stir. If more bread crumbs are needed, add a little at a time. If you put too much, add a little water. Stuff into mushroom caps. Sprinkle with cheese and broil 5-7 minutes.

Note: These make delicious appetizers.

PEAS

Peas and Cauliflower

1 pkg. frozen cauliflower
1 pkg. frozen peas
1/4 tsp. butter flavoring
1/4 tsp. pepper
2 Tbsp. chopped pimiento

Cook vegetables according to package directions. Stir in pimiento and season with salt and pepper. Serves 4.

Peas and Green Onions

2 pkgs. cooked peas
2 bunches green onions, thinly sliced
1 tsp. margarine
2 tsp. flour
dash of sweetener, *optional*
salt and pepper to taste
1/4 tsp. ground nutmeg

Cook peas, adding onions and margarine during last two minutes to soften. Drain vegetables, saving 3/4 cup water; add extra water, if needed. Add flour to cooking water and make a paste; cook slowly, stirring until thickened. Add vegetables and seasonings. Serves 4.

Springtime Peas

2 lbs. fresh peas *or* 2 pkgs. frozen peas
3-6 moist lettuce leaves
1/3 cup sliced green onion
1/2 tsp. salt
dash of pepper
1/4 tsp. thyme
1 tsp. snipped parsley
1 tsp. margarine

Shell peas, if fresh. Cover bottom of a 10" skillet with lettuce leaves. Top with peas and onion. Sprinkle with seasonings. Cover tightly and cook over low heat 10-15 minutes or until peas are tender. Remove lettuce leaves. Drain peas, adjust seasonings, and dot with margarine.

Quick Creole Peas

1 10-oz. pkg. frozen peas
1/2 cup chopped onion
1/4 cup chopped green pepper
5 tsp. diet margarine
1 large tomato, crushed
1/2 tsp. salt
1/4 tsp. pepper

Cook peas according to package directions; drain. Cook onion and green pepper in margarine until tender but not brown. Reserve 2 Tbsp. tomato liquid. Cut tomatoes in pieces and add to cooked onion. Stir in salt, pepper, and the drained peas. Heat mixture to boiling. Stir tomato liquid into peas. Cook and stir until mixture thickens and boils.

Note: 1/2 cup = 1 serving.
Cheryl Doyle

Minted Peas

1 tsp. margarine
1/2 cup chopped onion
2 pkgs. frozen peas
2 Tbsp. water
1 Tbsp. finely chopped fresh mint leaves or 1/2 tsp. peppermint extract
1 tsp. lemon juice
1/2 tsp. salt

Melt margarine in a non-stick skillet and sauté onions until tender. Add remaining ingredients. Cover pan and simmer 7-8 minutes until tender. Add water if necessary to prevent sticking or burning.

Note: In microwave, peas take 5-6 minutes to cook.

Peas and Green Grapes

1 cup green peas, cooked
12 seedless green grapes
1 tsp. margarine
salt and pepper to taste
pinch of dried tarragon

Combine green peas and green grapes. Heat margarine in a pan; add peas and grapes. Stir over medium-high heat until they are just heated through. Add salt, pepper, and tarragon.

Note: Green seedless grapes add a quick gourmet touch to green peas whether the peas are canned, frozen, or fresh. This combination is especially nice with fish or chicken.
Cheryl Doyle

PEPPERS

Stuffed Pepper Boats

6 green peppers, washed, seeded, and halved
1 lb. cottage cheese
1/4 cup diced dill pickles
1/2 cup diced celery (with tops)
1 whole pimiento, diced
salt and pepper to taste
chives or leeks

Pat insides of green peppers dry. Put cottage cheese through sieve, or blend until smooth. Combine cottage cheese, pickles, celery, and diced pimiento. Stuff green peppers. Chill overnight; then cut into thirds. To make sailboats, cut 1 1/2" pieces of celery and secure to peppers with toothpicks.

Variation: The filling is delicious for deviled eggs, too. Simply mash hard-boiled yolks with cottage cheese mixture and stuff hard-cooked egg whites. Adjust quantity of filling as needed.

POTATOES

Parsleyed Potatoes

Idaho potatoes, washed
parsley
paprika
butter-salt

Bake potatoes with skin on until tender, and remove from oven. Slice 1/4" thin, layer in a dish, and sprinkle top with parsley, paprika, and butter salt. Keep warm until served. Allow 1/2 potato per serving.

Whipped Baked Potatoes

large Idaho potatoes
skim milk
butter-salt

Bake potatoes until tender. Cut in half lengthwise. Scoop interior out. Whip potato with small amount of skim milk to desired consistency and add 1/8 tsp. butter-flavored salt for each potato half. Pile attractively back into shell and sprinkle with paprika. Allow 1/2 potato per person.

Variation: Add Parmesan cheese on top.

SPINACH

Cheesy Spinach (Microwaved)

1 Tbsp. margarine
1 10-oz. pkg. frozen chopped spinach
1/3 cup cottage cheese
1/2 tsp. salt
2 oz. grated Muenster cheese
2 slices whole wheat bread, crumbed
2 eggs, beaten
1 1/2 tsp. instant minced onion
dash of pepper

Place margarine in a bowl, set in microwave, and heat 1 minute until melted. Stir in bread crumbs and 2 Tbsp. shredded cheese. Cook 1 minute. Set aside. Cook spinach in a 1 1/2-qt. casserole for 5 minutes or until cooked; drain and return to casserole. Stir in remaining ingredients. Cook on high 6 minutes, stirring every 2 minutes or until mixture thickens. Sprinkle bread crumb mixture on top. Cook 2 minutes. Serve immediately. Makes 4 servings.

Spinach Sesame

1 1/2 lbs. fresh spinach, washed
1/2 tsp. butter-salt
2 Tbsp. toasted sesame seeds*

*Toast seeds by sprinkling them on a cookie sheet and baking at 400° until brown. Watch carefully to avoid burning.

Place spinach in pan with just enough water clinging to leaves and add salt. Cook spinach uncovered over moderate heat until tender. Sprinkle with sesame seeds.

SQUASH

Baked Acorn Squash

1 acorn squash, halved and seeded
dash of butter-salt
dash of cinnamon
brown sugar sweetener
chopped apples
walnuts

Sprinkle squash with butter-salt, cinnamon, and sweetener. Bake shell side up for about 45 minutes. Remove and stuff with chopped apples and walnuts. Bake for 30 minutes or until apples are done. Sprinkle with additional cinnamon and sugar, if desired.

Grilled Summer Squash

summer squash
butter flavoring
salt and pepper to taste
dash of garlic powder

Slice squash onto squares of doubled aluminum foil. Season with butter flavoring, salt, pepper, and garlic powder. Seal and grill over medium fire 10-15 minutes or until tender.

Spicy Apple-Squash Bake

acorn or butternut squash halves, seeded
butter flavoring
1/2 cup unsweetened applesauce per squash half
dash of nutmeg
dash of cinnamon

Bake squash halves 40 minutes at 350° or until tender. Brush center with butter flavoring. Fill each cavity with 1/2 cup applesauce. Sprinkle with nutmeg and cinnamon; return to oven until warm.

Herbed Zucchini

1 1/2 lbs. or 6 medium zucchini
1/2 tsp. salt
1 tsp. mixed salad herbs*
1/2 cup water

*chopped parsley, chives, basil, rosemary, or other herbs as desired.

Trim zucchini; halve each crosswise. Make 4-5 cuts in each half, starting at wide end and cutting almost to tip. Combine with salt, herbs, and water in a medium frying pan; cover. Cook 10 minutes or until tender-crisp; drain. Place on heated serving plates; spread cuts to form a fan. Makes 6 servings.

Stuffed Zucchini

10 zucchini, sliced lengthwise
1 cup spinach
1 cup bean sprouts
4 cups beef bouillon
paprika

Parboil zucchini in bouillon (skin should remain firm). Cook spinach and bean sprouts until tender. Scoop out zucchini, leaving shells. Blend spinach and bean sprouts until smooth. Spoon this mixture into shells. Sprinkle with paprika. Bake at 350° for 10-12 minutes. Serves 10.

Note: These are good, hot or cold.

Swiss Onion and Zucchini Bake
(Microwave)

1 Tbsp. margarine
3 cups thinly sliced onion
2 medium zucchini, thinly sliced
2 eggs
1/4 cup milk
1 tsp. salt
1/2 tsp. dry mustard
dash of pepper
1 cup or 4 oz. grated Swiss cheese

Melt margarine in a flat 1 1/2-qt. dish. Stir in onion and zucchini; cover with waxed paper. Microwave on high for 6-7 minutes or until tender, stirring once after 4 minutes. Stir together eggs, milk, salt, dry mustard, pepper, and half the cheese. Pour mixture over vegetables. Sprinkle with remaining cheese. Cover with paper towel. Microwave on medium for 8-10 minutes or until firm. Serves 6.

Variation: Bake at 350° for 35 minutes, if preferred.

Zucchini Italiano

1 cup tomato juice
1 Tbsp. dehydrated onion flakes
1/8 tsp. garlic powder
1/4 tsp. salt
dash of pepper
1/4 tsp. basil leaves
1/8 tsp. powdered thyme
1 medium zucchini
1 small jar mushrooms, sliced
1 oz. grated Parmesan cheese
1 oz. grated Romano cheese

1 egg, beaten
salt and pepper
1/4 tsp. oregano

In a small skillet, combine first 7 ingredients and cook over medium heat until thick. Slice zucchini 1/4" thick and cook in tomato sauce for 5 minutes. Add drained mushrooms and cook covered 5 minutes longer, with zucchini still crisp. Sprinkle half the grated cheese over top. Beat egg and season with salt, pepper, and oregano. Then pour over top of cheese. Let egg spread over top; do not stir. Sprinkle with remaining cheese. Cover and cook over low heat about 3 minutes, until egg is cooked and cheese melted. Serves one.

Zucchini Provençal

1 Tbsp. margarine
1 medium onion, chopped
1 clove garlic, minced
3 zucchini, sliced
2 tomatoes, peeled and chopped
1 tsp. salt
1/4 tsp. oregano
pepper to taste

In a large skillet, melt margarine. Add onion and garlic; cook until tender about 5 minutes. Add zucchini and remaining ingredients. Mix well, cover, and cook over moderately low heat for 10-15 minutes, or until zucchini is tender-crisp. Serves 4.

SWEET POTATOES

Mock Sweet Potatoes

1 lb. fresh butternut squash
1/2 cup orange juice
sweetener to equal 1 tsp. sugar
dash of nutmeg
dash of cinnamon
orange slices

Peel squash. Boil in orange juice until tender. Mash well. Add sweetener, nutmeg, and cinnamon. Spoon into casserole. Bake at 350° for 30 minutes. Garnish with orange slices.

TOMATOES

Middle Eastern Stuffed Tomatoes

1 large eggplant
2 Tbsp. minced green onions
1 clove garlic, minced
1/2 tsp. salt
1/2 tsp. pepper
1 Tbsp. lemon juice
4 medium ripe tomatoes
parsley sprigs
lemon wedges

Cut eggplant in half lengthwise and broil skin side up until skin is charred and eggplant is tender. Scoop out pulp, and chop it coarsely. In a medium-sized bowl, combine onions, garlic, salt, pepper, and lemon juice. Cut a 1/4" slice from top of each tomato. Scoop out pulp with a teaspoon. Sprinkle insides of shells with salt; then turn them upside down on paper toweling to drain. Arrange tomatoes on a serving platter. Fill with eggplant mixture. Garnish tomatoes with parsley sprigs and lemon wedges. Serve chilled.

Variation: Use pulp in soup, stew, or mixed vegetable combinations. Bake eggplant whole in 425° oven for 1/2 hour or until tender.

Cheryl Doyle

Peppy Tomato Slices

6 medium tomatoes, sliced
1/2 green pepper, finely diced
1 small onion, finely diced
2 Tbsp. fresh parsley
3 Tbsp. vegetable oil
6 Tbsp. vinegar
1 tsp. horseradish
1/2 tsp. paprika
1/2 tsp. dry mustard
1/4 tsp. celery powder
1/4 tsp. salt

Slice tomatoes at least 1/4" thick. Overlap in shallow dish. Combine remaining ingredients in a jar and shake. Pour over tomatoes. Cover and refrigerate several hours. Yields 6 servings at 60 calories per serving.

Ratatouille

3 tsp. oil
3 tsp. water
1 medium bell pepper, cut
  lengthwise 1/4" thick
1/4 lb. medium mushrooms, sliced
  lengthwise
1/2 cup onion, thinly sliced
1 clove garlic, crushed
2 medium yellow squash, cut
  diagonally 1/4" thick

1 medium eggplant, unpeeled and quartered lengthwise
2 medium tomatoes, peeled and cut into wedges
1/2 tsp. salt
1/2 tsp. pepper
1 Tbsp. chopped parsley

With oil and water in medium skillet, sauté green pepper, mushrooms, onion, and garlic for 5 minutes, or until onion is transparent. With slotted spoon, transfer to medium bowl. Cut eggplant crosswise 1/4" thick. Sauté separately squash 10 minutes and eggplant 5 minutes in skillet, each time transferring cooked squash and eggplant to bowl. Return previously sautéed vegetables to same skillet. Layer 1/2 the tomato wedges on top. Sprinkle with salt, pepper, and 1/2 tsp. parsley. Stir gently to mix. Layer remaining tomato on top. Sprinkle with another 1/2 tsp. parsley. Simmer covered mixture over low heat for 10 minutes. Remove cover; cook, basting occasionally with pan juices, 5 minutes longer or until liquid is evaporated. Turn into large, shallow serving dish. Sprinkle with remaining parsley. Serves 8-10.
Cheryl Doyle

Tomatoes Stuffed with Eggplant and Zucchini

1 large ripe tomato
1/2 cup chopped zucchini
1/2 cup coarsely grated eggplant
pinch of oregano
pinch of basil

salt and pepper to taste
sweetener to equal 1 tsp. sugar
2 tsp. minced parsley
1 tsp. vegetable oil, *optional*

Slice top off tomato and discard. Scoop out pulp and put pulp in medium pan. Add zucchini, eggplant, oregano, and basil. Sauté until vegetables are soft. Meanwhile, season tomato shell with salt, pepper, and sweetener. Broil tomato 4" from heat in preheated broiler for 4-5 minutes or until shell is softened. Sprinkle inside with 1 tsp. parsley. Add cooked vegetables and bake at 450° for 10-15 minutes. Drizzle oil over all, if desired. Garnish with remaining parsley. Serves one person.

Tropical Tomatoes

1 large tomato
1 small green-tipped banana
salt
paprika
1 oz. Muenster cheese, grated

Remove stem end from tomato, and cut tomato into 4 slices crosswise. Peel banana and cut into thin slices. Put tomato slices on heat-proof platter. Top with overlapping circles of banana slices. Sprinkle with salt, paprika, and grated cheese. Broil about 5" from heat for 10 minutes or until cheese is melted and tomatoes are slightly cooked. Serve immediately.
Cheryl Doyle

TURNIPS

Lemon Parsleyed Turnips

2 cups turnip sticks
2 tsp. diet margarine
2 tsp. snipped parsley
1 tsp. finely chopped onion
1 tsp. lemon juice

Cook turnip sticks in boiling salted water for 20 minutes *or* until tender; drain. Add margarine, parsley, onion, and lemon juice. Toss. Serves 4.

VEGETABLE MELANGE

Beefy Vegetables

1/2 cup water
1 beef bouillon cube
1 pkg. frozen vegetables

Boil water in saucepan. Add bouillon cube and vegetables, separating with a fork. Heat liquid to boiling,. Lower heat and simmer until tender. Serves 3.

Cold Vegetables á la Grecque

Marinade:
3 cups chicken stock, fresh *or* canned
1/4 cup red wine vinegar
2 tsp. olive oil
10 coriander seeds, bruised slightly
10 peppercorns, bruised slightly
2 large cloves garlic, thinly sliced
2 tsp. salt
1/4 tsp. thyme
4 sprigs parsley

1 large bay leaf
1/2 cup lemon juice

Vegetables:
2 stalks fennel, if available
20 small white onions, peeled carefully
2 zucchini, unpeeled and sliced 1" thick
3 yellow squash, unpeeled and sliced 1" thick
4 peppers, cut lengthwise into 1/2" strips
2 Tbsp. finely chopped parsley
lemon slices

Combine marinade ingredients in a 3-4-qt. pan; bring to a boil. Cover pan tightly and reduce heat. Simmer *slowly* for 45 minutes. Strain through sieve into mixing bowl; press vegetables to extract their juices before throwing them away. Return marinade to saucepan and adjust salt. Cook vegetables separately in marinade. Bring marinade to a boil. Drop onions in and cover. Reduce heat to moderate and boil 30 minutes or so, checking periodically for doneness. Using a slotted spoon, transfer to large shallow baking dish. Next, do the squash and zucchini, using the boiling procedure for approximately 15 minutes. Boil peppers last, in uncovered pot for only 8 minutes. Pour marinade over vegetables in baking dish; be sure each piece is partially immersed in hot liquid. Cool. Then cover dish with plastic wrap and refrigerate 12 hours. Arrange vegetables on large round platter. Moisten vegetables with a few spoonfuls of marinade, sprinkle with parsley, and arrange lemon slices around the edge. Delightful!

Marinated Vegetables

1 1/2 cups green beans, cut in pieces
1/2 cup mushrooms, stems, and pieces
3 Tbsp. dehydrated onion flakes
1 cucumber, sliced
1/2 cup pimientos, sliced
1/2 cup radishes, sliced
1 cup zucchini, sliced
2 cups cauliflower, cut in small pieces
Marinade:
1/2 cup wine vinegar
1/2 cup water
pepper, *optional*
sweetener to equal 2 tsp. sugar
1 1/2 tsp. seasoned salt
1/2 tsp. garlic powder

Combine vegetables. Prepare marinade and pour over vegetables. Refrigerate overnight.

Southern Vegetables

1 medium white turnip, diced
1 onion, diced
1/4 head cabbage, shredded
1/2 pkg. frozen chopped cauliflower
1 small zucchini, diced
1/4 tsp. dried marjoram
1 small rutabaga, diced
1 carrot, diced
1/2 pkg. frozen chopped broccoli
1 large tomato, chopped
2 qts. water
1/4 tsp. dried basil
grated Swiss cheese

Place turnip, onion, rutabaga, and carrot in deep soup pot with a small amount of water to cover vegetables. Cover and simmer until partially tender. Add all remaining ingredients. Cover and simmer gently for 40 minutes. Before serving, add grated Swiss cheese on top.

Spring Vegetable Medley

1 10-oz. pkg. frozen peas
1 8-oz. can water chestnuts, sliced
2 Tbsp. powdered chicken bouillon
1 Tbsp. cornstarch
1/2 tsp. seasoned salt
1/4 tsp. garlic powder
1/2 cup water
2 Tbsp. margarine
1 cup halved cherry tomatoes

In a 1 1/2-qt. casserole, place peas and water chestnuts. In small bowl, stir together bouillon, cornstarch, seasoned salt, and garlic powder. Sprinkle over vegetables and toss to coat. Pour water over and dot with margarine. Cover and bake at 400° for 20 minutes. Stir in tomatoes, cover, and continue cooking an additional 5 minutes. Serves 2.

Vegetable K-Bobs

small onions
cherry tomatoes
green pepper chunks
fresh pineapple chunks
fresh whole mushrooms

Alternate vegetables on skewers. Bake in 350° oven or cook over grill approximately 1 hour.

Main Dishes
&
Sauces

How often do you associate main dishes with *meat* dishes? Some habits die hard, especially when it comes to meat. Both my father and grandfather were butchers, so meat at every meal was commonplace. It took me several years to gradually learn to cook less of it.

Most nutritionists agree that many Americans consume more meat than is needed for their health. If I had my way, I'd have everyone planning the meal around vegetables, with meat as a side dish or a condiment to flavor the vegetables!

Take no thought for your life, what ye shall eat, or what ye shall drink. . . . Is not the life more than meat? . . .

Matthew 6:25 (KJV)

The verse doesn't mean we shouldn't think about what we put in our mouths. As temples of God, we should care about health and food, but not make them the whole point of our existence!

POINTERS TO HEALTHFUL EATING

Main dishes, as the heart of a meal, generally provide the basic protein intake. One ounce of protein has about 75 calories. Several ounces of meat add up quickly!

In a calorie-controlled diet, women are permitted 1000-1200 calories per day, while men may have 1500. According to the American Heart Association, the YMCA Slim Living Program, the Senate Select Committee on Nutrition, and the Diabetes Association, 5 to 6 ounces of protein per day is adequate. In the Slim Living classes, the protein is divided up as follows:

Breakfast: 1 ounce
Lunch: 2 ounces
Dinner: 3-4 ounces

Things to consider about portions:

(1) Cheeses and eggs: one egg equals 1 ounce of protein. Limit eggs to four a week or less.

Swiss and Muenster cheeses have 110 calories per ounce.

1/2 cup cottage cheese is one protein portion.

(2) Poultry: excellent protein source, except for the fatty skin which should be removed.

(3) Beef, Pork, and Lamb: generally high in fat and good to mix into vegetable casseroles. Limit to no more than 12 ounces per week.

(4) Fish: low in fat content, unless fried.

(5) Bread, Potatoes, and Rice: starchy, so limit your intake of these.

Casserole Toppers

Decorate the tops of casseroles for an extra special touch. These add extra calories, so indulge sparingly!

Edge them with a ring of shredded cheese.

Adorn them with prebaked pastry cutouts or small biscuits.

Add buttered bread crumbs, crushed chow mein noodles or crackers around the edges.

BEEF

Beef and Sauerkraut Casserole

1 lb. ground beef
1 can sauerkraut, drained
2 tsp. onion flakes
1/4 tsp. parsley
1 green pepper, chopped
2 stalks celery, sliced
2 cups tomato juice

Cook and drain beef. Add remaining ingredients. Put into a 1 1/2-qt. casserole and bake at 350° for 1 1/2 hours.

Beef and Sprout Casserole

4 oz. ground beef
1/2 tsp. onion powder
3 cans bean sprouts, rinsed and drained
1 4-oz. can mushrooms
2 oz. Mozzarella cheese, grated

Sauce:
2 cups tomato juice
1/2 tsp. garlic powder
pinch of whole oregano flakes
1/2 tsp. parsley flakes

1/8 tsp. Italian seasoning

Sauté meat with onion powder; drain off fat. In casserole dish, alternately layer meat, sprouts, mushrooms, and cheese. Combine sauce ingredients and cook on medium-low heat until thick. Then pour sauce over cheese; poke holes through layers so juice penetrates.

Gloria Ayers

Beef and Sprout Hash

2 large onions, diced
2 green peppers, diced
1 Tbsp. shortening or oil
1/2 lb. ground beef
2 cups canned tomatoes
1 cup cooked sprouts
1 tsp. chili powder
1 tsp. salt
1/2 tsp. pepper

Sauté onions and green peppers in shortening until soft. Add ground beef and cook. Drain fat. Add tomatoes, sprouts, and seasonings. Place in casserole and bake at 375° for 45 minutes. Serves 4.

Beef and Zucchini Bake

4 oz. lean hamburger
1/2 cup chopped onions
1 cup chopped celery
1 cup tomato juice
dash of *each:*
  garlic or garlic powder
  oregano
  parsley
  basil

1 bay leaf
pepper to taste
1 medium zucchini

Brown first 3 ingredients. Add juice and seasonings. Simmer for 1 1/2 to 2 hours. Slice zucchini into a 1-qt. casserole. Pour sauce over and bake at 400° for 45 minutes. Serves 1.

Variation: Place chopped spinach on bottom of casserole with zucchini. Add 4 oz. cubed Muenster or Swiss cheese on top during last 10 minutes of baking. Serves 2.

Beef Vegetable Pie

1 egg, slightly beaten
1/2 cup tomato juice
1 tsp. salt
1 tsp. onion powder
1/2 tsp. chili powder
1/4 tsp. pepper
1 cup crunchy bran cereal
1 lb. ground round
1 10-oz. pkg. frozen mixed vegetables
1/2 cup grated Swiss or Muenster
  cheese

In a medium bowl, combine first 6 ingredients. Stir in cereal to coat. Let stand 5 minutes. Break up mixture. Add beef and mix well. Press gently into pie plate, shaping to fit. Toss cooked vegetables with 1/2 the cheese. Turn into beef shell. Sprinkle remaining cheese over vegetables. Bake at 350° for 30 minutes. Let stand 5-10 minutes to set. Serves 6.

Variation: Try different vegetables in this recipe.

Betty's Campy Lasagna

1/4 cup minced onion
1 lb. lean ground beef
8 oz. tomato sauce
1 tsp. basil
1 tsp. parsley
dash of garlic powder
salt and pepper to taste
4 oz. mushrooms, drained
1 10-oz. pkg. frozen chopped
  spinach, thawed and drained
6 oz. cottage cheese
4 oz. Mozzarella cheese, cut in strips

Sauté onions and beef. Drain fat and add tomato sauce, seasonings, and mushrooms. Combine spinach and cottage cheese. Layer spinach mixture, meat mixture, and cheese in a 2-qt. casserole. Bake at 350° for 20 minutes. Makes 4-5 servings of protein.

Lasagna Surprise

1 medium head cabbage, sliced
3 cups vegetable or tomato juice
2 tsp. beef bouillon
1 lb. lean ground beef
2 Tbsp. onion flakes
1 Tbsp. paprika
4 tsp. Italian seasoning or 1 tsp. each:
  oregano
  basil
  sage
  savory
1/2 tsp. fennel seed or anise
4 medium cloves garlic or 1/2 tsp.
  garlic powder
salt and pepper to taste
12 oz. cottage cheese or ricotta
1 oz. Parmesan cheese, grated

1/4 cup chopped parsley
1 egg
3 oz. Mozzarella, shredded

Cook sliced cabbage in juice and bouillon. Drain, reserving liquid. Set both aside. Sauté ground beef; drain. To beef, add onion flakes, reserved liquid, and seasonings, except parsley. Cook down to desired thickness. Combine cottage cheese, Parmesan, parsley, and egg. Alternate layers of meat, Mozzarella, cabbage, and cottage cheese mixture. Save some Mozzarella for top. Bake at 350° for 30-40 minutes.

Note: 1 oz. of cheese is equivalent to 1/4 cup.

Judy Booster

Shepherd's Pie Casserole

4 oz. ground beef
1/2 cup water
1 small can mushrooms, drained and
  chopped
4 oz. carrots, sliced
4 oz. onions, sliced
salt and pepper to taste
1 pkg. frozen cauliflower, thawed
2 Tbsp. instant milk powder

Broil ground beef. Add water, mushrooms, carrots, onions, salt, and pepper. Cook cauliflower until barely tender. Put in blender with cooking liquid and milk powder. Blend slightly. Put ground beef mixture in a Pam-sprayed casserole, and top with cauliflower. Bake at 400° for 30 minutes.

Chili

1 lb. ground beef
salt and pepper to taste
2 cups tomato juice
1/2 head cabbage, shredded
1 tsp. chili powder
1/2 green pepper
1/4 tsp. onion powder

Salt and pepper meat and broil until done. Place meat in casserole dish with remaining ingredients. Bake at 350° for 30 minutes.

Variation: Use veal instead of beef.

Cabbage Chili

1 lb. lean ground beef
2 medium tomatoes, chopped
4 oz. fresh onion, chopped
1/2 tsp. oregano
2 tsp. chili powder
1 cup tomato juice
1/2 head cabbage, grated
dash of garlic powder
1/2 green pepper, chopped

Broil beef, drain fat, and put in saucepan with other ingredients. Simmer at least 30 minutes. Serves 4.

Hearty Hodgepodge

1 lb. ground beef
1 onion, chopped
1 green pepper, diced
1 16-oz. can tomatoes
sweetener to equal 1 Tbsp. sugar
1 1/2 tsp. salt
1/2 tsp. pepper
1/2 tsp. garlic powder

1 8-oz. can green beans
1 8-oz. can peas, drained
1 4-oz. can mushrooms, drained

Brown ground beef in skillet over medium heat. Drain well. Combine with all remaining ingredients and add to crock pot. Stir well. Cover and cook on low 6-8 hours.

Oriental Beef Skillet

1 lb. lean ground beef
1 onion, chopped
1/2 cup chopped celery
1 can Chinese vegetables *or* 1/2 can water chestnuts
1/2 can bamboo shoots
1 can mushrooms
1/4 tsp. ginger
3 Tbsp. soy sauce
sweetener to equal 1 tsp. sugar
arrowroot

Cook beef, onion, and celery in a non-stick pan until vegetables are tender-crisp. Add remaining vegetables. Cook 20 minutes; then add ginger, soy sauce, and sweetener. Thicken with arrowroot. Serve with extra bean sprouts or rice.

Carrot Burgers

1 lb. ground beef
2 cups shredded carrots
1 onion, chopped
1 tsp. salt
1/4 tsp. pepper
1 tsp. soy sauce

Combine ingredients and shape into patties. Broil until done. Great over charcoal!

"Tacos"

8 oz. ground beef
1 tsp. chili powder
1 tsp. dehydrated onion flakes
1/4 tsp. salt
1/4 tsp. onion powder
1/4 tsp. paprika
dash of red hot sauce
1 slice bread
1/2 cup shredded lettuce
1 Tbsp. pimiento
1 tsp. mustard
1 tsp. vinegar

Brown meat. Add seasonings and cook 5 minutes. Remove from pan. Toast bread lightly. Spread meat mixture on 1/2 a slice. Fold bread and hold in place with toothpicks. Combine remaining ingredients and add to top of meat mixture.

Variation: Use ground veal instead of beef.

Cabbage-Rolled Franks

1 small head cabbage
1 lb. all-beef franks
2 cups tomato juice
2 Tbsp. prepared mustard
1 Tbsp. onion flakes
1 Tbsp. Worcestershire sauce
1/8 tsp. black pepper

Boil cabbage leaves until softened; set aside one leaf per frank. Cook remaining cabbage until done; then dice. Put in bottom of a 2-qt. casserole. Roll leaves around franks and set on top of diced cabbage. Combine last five ingredients and pour over and around franks. Bake at 350° for 45 minutes.

Variation: Use turkey *or* chicken franks for a change.

Pineapple-Frankfurter Kabobs

1 lb. all-beef franks
5 slices pineapple
1/2 cup pineapple juice
1/4 green pepper, diced
1 tsp. mustard
paprika

Cut franks in 1" chunks; add to pineapple juice along with mustard and green pepper in a pan; bring to a boil and cook 5 minutes. Remove meat from juice, and place alternately with pineapple on toothpick or skewer. Garnish with green pepper and paprika. Serves 4.

Variation: Use pineapple chunks. Try turkey or chicken franks.

Mushroom Hamburger Grill

2 oz. onion, finely diced
8 oz. ground beef
4 oz. mushrooms, finely diced
salt and pepper to taste
2 oz. French-style green beans, finely mashed
2 oz. tomato juice
1/8 tsp. garlic powder

Mix all ingredients together. Form patties and broil. Great over charcoal!

Meatballs and "Spaghetti"

1 lb. ground beef

Sauce:
8 oz. tomato juice
4 oz. onion, diced
1 clove garlic, diced *or* 1/2 tsp.
    garlic powder
dash of salt and pepper
dash of oregano
1 tsp. dehydrated parsley
1/2 tsp. basil
1 can bean sprouts, drained
1 can mushrooms, drained

Roll ground beef into small balls (wet hands with ice water so beef won't stick). Place beef balls on meat rack. Broil slightly. Put in large pan with sauce ingredients. Cook 1 hour on low heat, stirring occasionally. Heat bean sprouts and mushrooms 5 minutes before serving with meatballs.

Meatballs Española

Meatballs:
1 lb. ground beef
2 Tbsp. onion flakes
1 tsp. Italian seasoning
1/2 tsp. garlic powder
salt and pepper to taste

Spaghetti Sauce:
1 46-oz. can tomato juice
2 bouillon cubes
pinch of onion powder
2 tsp. oregano
1 bay leaf
1 tsp. parsley

pinch of basil
4 zucchini

Make meatballs and broil; then drain on paper towels. Mix sauce ingredients together and simmer until thickened. Remove bay leaf. Slice zucchini into a 13" x 9" x 2" pan, filling pan half full. Cover zucchini with spaghetti sauce. Place meatballs on top of zucchini and cover pan with foil. Bake at 350° for about 45 minutes or until zucchini are done. Serve with grated Parmesan cheese if desired.

Judy Booster

Sweet and Sour Meatballs

1 lb. ground beef
1 Tbsp. prepared mustard
1/2 cup dehydrated onion flakes
2 cups tomato juice
1/4 cup vinegar
1/4 cup soy sauce
1/4 tsp. garlic powder
sweetener to equal 1/4 cup sugar
4 slices pineapple
4 Tbsp. pineapple juice

Combine beef, mustard, and onion flakes. Mix well. Shape into balls and bake at 350° for 15 minutes or until done. Combine remaining ingredients. Bring to a boil and add meatballs. Simmer 4 minutes or until thoroughly heated.

Betty's Meat Loaf

2 lbs. ground chuck
1/2 cup oatmeal
1/4 cup skim milk
1 medium onion, finely chopped
1 cup chopped sauerkraut, drained
1 Tbsp. salt
2 eggs
1 cup tomato juice

Mix all ingredients with 1/2 the tomato juice. Place in a loaf pan. Pour remaining juice over meat. Cover and bake at 350° for 1 1/2 hours. Drain off fat. Serves 5-6.

Note: A heart-shaped pan would be great!

Simple Meat Loaf

1 lb. ground beef
1 1/2 Tbsp. horseradish
8 oz. tomato juice
1 Tbsp. chopped chives
salt and pepper to taste

Combine all ingredients and put in a Pam-sprayed loaf pan. Turn upside on sprayed grill (or well-punctured piece of heavy foil); if baking in oven, place another pan below. Bake at 350° for 45 minutes to 1 hour. Leave loaf pan over meat while baking to retain moisture. Serve hot.

Barbecued Beef on Skewers

Marinade:
1/2 cup vinegar
1 garlic clove, chopped
1 Tbsp. chopped chili pepper
1 tsp. powdered cumin
1/2 tsp. salt

1 8-oz. steak
1 medium green pepper, cut in strips
1/2 cup whole mushrooms
black pepper

Combine marinade ingredients. Cut meat into bite-sized pieces and marinate 2 hours. Remove meat and place on skewer alternately with green pepper and mushrooms. Season with black pepper. Grill over charcoal until brown.

Variation: Chicken is a delicious substitute.

Barbecued Beef Supreme

1 lb. lean stew beef
1/2 large green pepper, chopped
1 stalk celery, chopped
1 small can mushrooms
1 tsp. dehydrated onions
salt and pepper to taste
garlic salt to taste
1/4 tsp. paprika
1 bay leaf
dash of soy sauce
1 tsp. beef bouillon
2 cups warm water
1 cup tomato juice

Place all ingredients in a large skillet. Cover and simmer about 2 hours or until beef is tender and juice is almost evaporated. Good with peas and cauliflower.

Beef Stew #1

1 1/2 lbs. beef, cut small
4 large carrots
3 onions, cut large
4 stalks celery
1 tsp. arrowroot or 1/2 tsp.
  cornstarch
salt and pepper to taste
1/2 cup tomato juice

Brown meat. Place meat and vegetables in a casserole dish. Mix remaining ingredients and add to meat and vegetables. Bake covered at 250° for 4 hours.

Note: This can also be put in a crock pot or slow cooker and cooked very slowly for a long time to enhance flavor.

Beef Stew #2

8 oz. ground chuck
1 cup tomato juice
4 oz. combined peas, carrots, and
  onions
1/2 cup French-style green beans
1/2 cup mushrooms

Brown meat and drain fat. Add remaining ingredients and simmer for 15 minutes. Serve alone or with cooked rice.

Savory Beef Stew

1 cup canned tomatoes
1 qt. water
parsley flakes
2 tsp. salt
1/4 tsp. pepper
1/2 tsp. paprika
1 cup chopped celery
1/4 cup chopped onions
2 lbs. beef, cut in 1" cubes
1 1/2 cups diced carrots

Mix tomatoes, water, seasonings, celery, and onions. Bring to a boil. Add meat and cook until partially tender. Add carrots and cook until meat and carrots are tender. Serve piping hot with dill pickles or your favorite condiment.

Variation: Use tomato juice instead of tomatoes.

Flank Steak

flank steak
1 medium carrot, diced
1 onion, chopped
2 bay leaves
1 tomato, chopped
1 tsp. thyme
1 cup water or stock
1/2 cup red wine vinegar

Brown meat in a non-stick deep, heavy casserole. Add next 5 ingredients and cook over medium heat for 5 minutes. Add last 2 ingredients. Bring to a boil, cover, and cook over low heat or in 350° oven. To serve, cut meat in 1/2" slices or serve cold on bed of lettuce with a slice of pickle.

Note: Adjust quantity of meat to number of people served.

Sukiyaki

1/4 lb. beef round steak, partially frozen
1/2 tsp. beef bouillon granules
1/4 cup boiling water
3 Tbsp. soy sauce
dash of sweetener, *optional*
2 tsp. cooking oil
3 cups thinly sliced celery cabbage
1 cup bias-sliced green onions
1/2 cup bias-sliced celery
8 oz. fresh tofu (bean curd), cubed
1 cup fresh bean sprouts
2 oz. bamboo shoots, drained
1/2 cup thinly sliced mushrooms
2 oz. water chestnuts, drained and sliced

Use partially frozen beef so it can be sliced very thin across grain into bite-sized pieces. Dissolve bouillon granules in boiling water; add soy sauce and sweetener. Preheat wok or pan; add oil. Add celery cabbage, green onions, and celery; stir fry 2 minutes. Add remaining ingredients; stir fry 1 minute. Remove vegetables. Add beef to hot pan and stir fry 1 minute. Stir in bouillon mixture; cook and stir until bubbly. Add vegetables. Cover and cook for 1 minute until heated through. Serve at once. Yields 2 servings.

Stuffed Flank Steak

Flank steak, thinly sliced
Stuffing #1:
1 1/2 Tbsp. margarine
1/4 cup finely chopped onion
1/4 cup finely chopped celery
1 large apple, pared, cored, and chopped
1 shallot, minced
1 Tbsp. chopped fresh parsley
1/2 tsp. chervil
pinch of thyme
1/4 tsp. sage
1/4 tsp. tarragon
salt and pepper to taste
1/2 cup coarse bread crumbs
1 egg white, beaten

Adjust quantity of meat to number of people served. Prepare meat for stuffing by pounding by hand or with mallet; then brown in sprayed, deep casserole.

Prepare either stuffing, using the same directions. Melt margarine in saucepan; add all but last 2 ingredients. Cook, uncovered over medium heat for 15 minutes, stirring occasionally. Adjust seasonings, as desired. Remove from heat. Add bread crumbs, mix well, and blend in egg white. Place 2 Tbsp. of stuffing in center of each steak and roll up, skewering with heavy cord. Prepare *Sauce.*

Stuffing #2:
1 1/2 Tbsp. margarine
1/2 lb. mushrooms, cleaned and minced
1 small onion, peeled and chopped
1 Tbsp. parsley, chopped fine
1 1/2 tsp. chervil
pinch of thyme
salt and pepper
1/8 tsp. fennel
1 drop Tabasco sauce

1/8 cup bread crumbs
1 egg white, beaten

Sauce:
1 small onion, minced
1 carrot, grated
2 bay leaves
1 tomato, chopped
pinch of thyme
1 cup water
1/2 cup red wine vinegar

Combine onion, carrot, bay leaves, tomato, and thyme. Cook over medium heat for 5 minutes. Then add water and vinegar. Bring to a boil. Cover meat and cook on very low for 1 1/2 hours or bake at 350° for 1 1/2 hours. To serve, cut in 1/2" pieces.

LAMB

Herbed Roast Shoulder of Lamb

4 1/2 lbs. lamb shoulder
salt and pepper to taste
6 bay leaves
1/2 tsp. thyme
1/2 tsp. rosemary
1/4 tsp. garlic powder
4 Tbsp. parsley
1/2 tsp. garlic powder

Roll and tie lamb securely. Sprinkle all seasonings on meat. Place meat in roaster and cook at 450° for 20 minutes; then lower heat to 375° and roast uncovered about 1 hour until tender. Remove bay leaves and serve.

Variation: Use veal instead of lamb.

Peppery Italian Roast Leg of Lamb

1 leg of lamb
1/4 cup lemon juice
dash of salt
1/4 tsp. oregano
1/4 tsp. crushed red pepper

Brush lamb with lemon juice; sprinkle lightly with salt and oregano. Sprinkle with red pepper, especially on fat side. Press pepper into meat. Place on rack in roasting pan. Roast at 325° for 30 minutes per pound or until meat thermometer registers 175° for medium doneness.

VEAL

"Spaghetti" and Veal

1 lb. ground veal
2 bouillon cubes
2 Tbsp. water
salt and pepper to taste
1/2 tsp. chili powder
1/2 tsp. basil
1/2 tsp. marjoram
2 cups tomato juice
1/2 tsp. onion powder
1 green pepper, cut up
1 tsp. garlic powder
1 tsp. oregano
1/2 tsp. parsley flakes
1 can bean sprouts, drained

Brown veal in bouillon and water. Add remaining ingredients, except bean sprouts. Simmer 1 hour. Drain bean sprouts and rinse. Add to sauce. Simmer 5 more minutes. Serve.

Hurry-Up Chili

8 oz. ground veal
3/4 cup tomato juice
1 small can mushrooms, drained
1 can French-style green beans,
    drained
2 tsp. chili powder
4 oz. onion, diced
salt and pepper to taste

Form veal patties and broil 5 minutes on each side. Crumble patties with fork and place in non-stick pan. Add remaining ingredients. Simmer for 30 minutes.

Veal Balls

1 1/2 lbs. ground veal
1 green pepper, diced
1 small onion, grated
salt and pepper to taste
cabbage leaves
1 small can tomato juice

Mix first 4 ingredients together and form into balls. Place in a 2-qt. baking dish. Bake at 400° until brown. Drain off all fat. Line bottom of dish with cabbage; add browned veal balls. Top with tomato juice and bake at 325° for 45 minutes.

Mary Ellen Pajak

Spanish Veal Barbecue

2 green peppers, diced
4 oz. onion, sliced and separated in
    rings
1 lb. fresh or canned mushrooms
8 oz. veal, cut in strips
pinch of paprika
1/2 tsp. dry mustard powder

1 tsp. sweetener
1/2 tsp. chili powder
1 1/2 Tbsp. white vinegar
1/4 cup water
1/4 tsp. marjoram
1/8 tsp. oregano
1/4 tsp. basil
1 cup tomato juice

Place green peppers and onions in non-stick skillet and simmer until soft. Add mushrooms and veal. Cook uncovered a few minutes, stirring occasionally to brown lightly. Add remaining ingredients. Simmer over low heat for 30 minutes or until sauce is thickened and veal is tender.

Veal Roll-Ups

1/2 tsp. soy sauce
1/2 cup water
1 can mushrooms, drained
2 stalks celery
2 stalks Chinese celery
1 green pepper, diced
2 oz. bamboo shoots, sliced
2 oz. water chestnuts, sliced
8 oz. veal, sliced

Steam vegetables in water and soy sauce until tender. Flatten out each piece of veal; stuff with cooked vegetables and roll up meat. Secure with toothpicks or string. Brown stuffed meat in liquid the vegetables were steamed in; baste frequently. Simmer in covered pot about 1 hour. Serve when veal is brown on all sides and tender.

Variation: Use 1/2 cup shredded cabbage, instead of Chinese celery.

Veal Veggies

8 oz. veal
4 oz. carrots, sliced
4 oz. onions
2 stalks celery
2 stalks Chinese cabbage with leaves
pinch of thyme
salt and pepper to taste

In a pot, alternately layer meat and vegetables. Cover with water; simmer covered 2 1/2 hours. Cool. Refrigerate and skim off fat. Reheat before serving.

POULTRY: CHICKEN

Almond Chicken Delight

1/4 cup thinly sliced almonds
1/2 cup thinly sliced carrots
1/2 tsp. dried dill weed
1 Tbsp. margarine
1/2 cup water
2 chicken bouillon cubes
2/3 cup instant milk powder
1 cup plain yogurt
2 5-oz. cans chunk white chicken or
    1 cup chopped, cooked chicken
paprika

In a saucepan, cook almonds and carrots with dill in margarine until tender. Blend in water, bouillon, milk powder, and yogurt. Add chicken. Heat and stir occasionally. Sprinkle with paprika. Serve plain, over toast, in pita bread, or over rice.

Chicken and Almonds

1/4 cup sliced almonds
1/4 cup thinly sliced carrots
1/2 tsp. dried dill weed
1 Tbsp. margarine
2 chicken bouillon cubes
2/3 cup instant milk powder
1/2 cup water
1/2 cup plain yogurt
1 cup cubed, cooked chicken
paprika

In a saucepan, brown almonds, carrots, and dill in margarine until tender. Blend in remaining ingredients; simmer for 5 minutes. Sprinkle with paprika and serve.

Chicken Ratatouille

8 oz. cooked, cut-up chicken
1 16-oz. can tomatoes
1 small eggplant, cut bite-sized
1 green pepper, sliced
1 onion, sliced
1 clove garlic, minced
dash of salt
dash of pepper
1 tsp. oregano
3 small zucchini, unpeeled

Combine all ingredients in a skillet. Heat to boiling. Reduce heat to low, cover, and simmer until vegetables are done.

Variation: Use turkey or shrimp. May be served over hot, mashed cauliflower, if desired.

Chicken and Carrot Surprise

1/2 baked chicken, cut up into
   1" chunks
4 stalks celery, cut
6 small carrots, sliced
1/2 tsp. butter flavoring
4 oz. orange juice
salt to taste
8 drops sweetener
2 Tbsp. cornstarch

Cook carrots and celery until tender in enough salt water to cover. Add butter flavoring and orange juice. Heat to boiling. Add salt, sweetener, and cornstarch to thicken. Add chicken to vegetable mixture. Serve over rice.

Chicken and Spinach

1 cup buttermilk
2 Tbsp. prepared mustard
8 oz. peas and onions, combined
12 oz. cooked chicken, diced
1/2 cup sliced pimiento
1 10-oz. pkg. frozen spinach

Gradually stir buttermilk into mustard. Cook peas and onions. Combine with chicken and pimiento. Cook over moderate heat until heated thoroughly. Cook spinach; drain. Serve chicken-vegetable mixture over spinach.

Chicken-Bean Casserole

4 cups French-style green beans
12 oz. chicken, cooked and diced
1 tsp. soy sauce
1 small can mushrooms, chopped
6 oz. skim milk
arrowroot
1 cup raw onions, diced

Spoon green beans into bottom of a non-stick 2 1/2-qt. casserole. Sprinkle evenly with diced chicken. Combine soy sauce, mushrooms, and milk; thicken with arrowroot, and mix well. Spoon over chicken. Cover with onions. Bake covered at 350° for 20 minutes. Uncover, baking for 10 minutes.

Chicken Chop Suey #1

1/2 cup thinly sliced onion
1/2 cup slivered green pepper
1 Tbsp. water
1 tsp. salt
1 cup slivered celery
1 cup sliced mushrooms
4 cups stock or bouillon
bean sprouts, canned or fresh
water chestnuts, optional
1 Tbsp. cornstarch
1 Tbsp. cold water
2 Tbsp. soy sauce
2 cups cooked, julienne-cut chicken

Sauté onions and green peppers in water with salt for 5 minutes. Add celery, mushrooms, and stock. Cover and cook slowly until celery is tender-crisp. Add bean sprouts and optional chestnuts. Mix cornstarch with cold water and add to mixture, stirring constantly. Add soy sauce and chicken. Serve with a tossed salad. Will keep for days and tastes better after it sits for a while.

Variations: Add other vegetables like broccoli or celery cabbage, if available. Use turkey instead of chicken.

Marilyn Rosenau

chicken. Place pineapple on top. Bake at 375° for 45 minutes.

Variation: Use turkey instead of chicken.

Chicken Chop Suey #2

1/2 small head cabbage
1 cup sliced cauliflower
1/2 can French-style green beans
1 can mushrooms
1/2 can water chestnuts, sliced
1/2 can bamboo shoots
2 cups tomato juice
2 Tbsp. soy sauce
dash of *each:*
　onion powder
　salt and pepper
　garlic salt
1 cup cooked chicken

Combine all ingredients except chicken; cook until tender. Then simmer for 1 hour. Add chicken and heat thoroughly.

Variation: Use shrimp instead of chicken.

Chicken 'n Stuffing

leftover chicken, cut in 1/2" slices
1 cup shredded carrots
1 cup shredded zucchini
1/4 tsp. poultry seasoning
5 slices canned *or* fresh pineapple

Line bottom of non-stick pan with sliced poultry. Combine carrots, zucchini, and poultry seasoning. Spoon over chicken. Layer with remaining

Swedish Fricassee

24 oz. cooked chicken, diced
8 oz. peas, drained
8 oz. carrots
1/2 cups celery, finely chopped
1/2 cup finely chopped green pepper
1 15-oz. can asparagus, drained
2 cups skim milk

Combine chicken, peas, carrots, celery, and green pepper. Combine asparagus and milk in blender; blend at high speed for 3 minutes. Put in saucepan and bring to a boil. Add chicken mixture. Cook 5 minutes.

Chicken Pot Pie

6 oz. chicken, cooked and cut up
3-4 stalks celery, chopped and
　cooked
4 oz. bean sprouts
8 oz. canned mushrooms, drained
1 1/2 cups chicken bouillon
arrowroot

Combine chicken, celery, bean sprouts, and mushrooms in a non-stick 8" square pan. Add bouillon and bake at 350° for 20-30 minutes. Then, add arrowroot to thicken.

Chicken Sprout Chili

3 cups tomato juice
1 tsp. onion flakes
1-2 tsp. chili powder
1 tsp. salt
8 oz. cooked chicken, chopped
1 16-oz. can bean sprouts, drained

Simmer tomato juice, onion flakes, chili powder, and salt until reduced to half. Add chicken and bean sprouts. Heat on top of stove or in the oven. Makes 2 servings.

Alpha Eckstein

Chicken Tetrazzini

1/2 tsp. margarine
1 cup chopped onion
1/2 cup chopped green pepper
1/4 cup chopped celery
2 cups skim milk
1 cup chicken bouillon
16 oz. cooked and diced chicken
2 cups cut-up bean sprouts
1 1/2 cups green beans, cooked
1 can mushrooms, drained
2 Tbsp. diced pimiento
salt and pepper to taste
1 slice bread, crumbed
1 oz. grated Swiss cheese

In a saucepan, sauté margarine, onion, green pepper, and celery. Gradually stir in milk and bouillon. Simmer until mixture comes to a boil. Remove from heat. Add all remaining ingredients except crumbs and cheese. Pour into a large casserole. Sprinkle bread crumbs and Swiss cheese on top. Bake at 400° for about 30 minutes.

Variation: Use turkey instead of chicken.

Piquant Chicken

3 cups chopped cabbage
1/2 cup chopped onion
1/2 cup chopped celery
1/2 cup chopped green pepper
1/2 cup chicken broth or bouillon
1 tsp. poultry seasoning
1 banana, sliced in 1 Tbsp. lemon juice
2 cups sugar-free applesauce
1 cup buttermilk
2 cups cooked and cubed chicken

Layer cabbage in bottom of a large casserole. Combine onion, celery, green pepper, and chicken broth; simmer until vegetables are tender. Then, add poultry seasoning, sliced banana, applesauce, and buttermilk. Layer chicken over cabbage, and top with vegetable mixture. Bake covered at 350° for 30 minutes and uncovered for 15 minutes.

Spanish Green Bean Scramble

4 oz. cooked turkey or chicken, chopped
1 Tbsp. chopped onion
1/2 medium tomato
1 Tbsp. chopped green pepper
1 tsp. margarine
1 16-oz. can French-style green beans, drained
salt and pepper to taste
1 egg

Sauté poultry with onion, tomato, and green pepper in margarine. Add drained beans, salt, and pepper. Simmer 10 minutes. Just before serving, break egg over mixture and scramble. Serves two.

Baked Chicken Liver Creole

1 lb. chicken liver
1 tsp. salt
1/4 cup chopped green pepper
2 tsp. chives
1/8 tsp. cayenne pepper
3/4 cup tomato juice

Sprinkle liver pieces with salt. Quickly brown in a non-stick pan over high heat, turning frequently. Put in baking dish. Combine remaining ingredients and pour over liver. Bake at 350° for 15 minutes.

Bar-B-Q Chicken

1 cup water
1 cup tomato juice
1/4 cup vinegar
1 tsp. salt
1 tsp. chili powder
1/4 cup Worcestershire sauce
1 Tbsp. liquid sweetener
1 Tbsp. celery salt
dash of hot sauce
6 pieces chicken thighs and legs

Mix together all ingredients, except chicken, and simmer for 1/2 hour. Place chicken in baking dish and cover with sauce. Bake at 350° for 1 hour or until chicken is tender. May also be cooked over coals.

Alma Zorn

Chicken and Vegetables

roasting chicken, cut up
seasoned salt and pepper
1 green pepper, chopped
1 Tbsp. onion flakes
4 chicken bouillon cubes
2 cups tomato juice
1/2 head cabbage, shredded
1/2 head cauliflower, cut up

Season chicken with seasoned salt and pepper. Add green pepper and onion flakes. Place in roaster with bouillon. Cover chicken with tomato juice. Bake, uncovered, at 350° for 1 1/4 hours. About 15 minutes before serving, add cabbage and cauliflower. Cook until tender.

Barb Nelson

Chicken Aloha

1 cup sugar-free pineapple-orange
   soda
1 tsp. soy sauce
1/2 cup diced celery
1/4 cup diced green pepper
1/2 tsp. ground ginger
salt and pepper to taste
2 chicken breasts, skinned
1/2 cup drained crushed pineapple
1 can bean sprouts

In a medium skillet, combine 1/2 cup soda, soy sauce, celery, green pepper, ginger, salt, and pepper. Add chicken breasts. Bring sauce to a boil; then reduce heat, cover, and simmer 35 minutes. Remove chicken breasts and add remaining soda, crushed pineapple, and bean sprouts to pan. Stir to moisten sprouts. Add chicken breasts, cover, and simmer 5 minutes. Serves 2.

Chicken Cacciatore

4 oz. onion, diced
1 2 1/2-lb. chicken, cut up and
    skinned
dash of paprika
8 oz. tomato juice
dash of salt
2 green peppers, sliced
1/2 lb. fresh or canned mushrooms
1 bay leaf, crushed
dash of oregano
1 can bean sprouts, drained

Cook diced onion in small amount of water until tender; drain. Season chicken with paprika and brown in a pot. Add bay leaf, tomato juice, salt, peppers, mushrooms, and oregano. Simmer for 1 hour, covered. When tender, uncover for last 5 minutes of cooking. Add bean sprouts to accent Italian flavor.

Chicken Paprika #1

1 medium onion
2 Tbsp. water
1/8 tsp. paprika
dash of cayenne pepper
dash of garlic powder
1 1/2 to 2 lbs. chicken, cut up
1 qt. canned tomatoes

In large saucepan, sauté onions in water. Add paprika, cayenne, and garlic. Add chicken and brown. Add tomatoes and simmer for 1 1/2-2 hours or until chicken is tender. Serve over rice, bean sprouts, or cooked cauliflower.

Variation: Use 3 lbs. cut-up beef instead of chicken.

Hunky Lou

Chicken Paprika #2

1 broiler, cut up
1 cup diced onion
1/4 tsp. garlic powder
1 cup chicken bouillon
2 tomatoes, chopped
1 tsp. paprika
1 can mushrooms, drained
1 can bean sprouts, drained

In a large non-stick pan, brown chicken, onions, and garlic powder. Simmer covered about 45 minutes. Add chicken broth, tomatoes, and paprika. Simmer and add 1 can drained mushrooms and bean sprouts.

Chicken Roll-Up

1 1/2 tsp. chives
1 1/2 tsp. margarine
1/2 slice toasted bread, crumbed .
1 chicken breast, rolled and boned
milk

Mix together chives and margarine and form into finger-length rolls. Place in freezer for 5 minutes. Place bread crumbs in shallow baking dish, distributing evenly; bake in 350° oven for 6-10 minutes until brown. Roll chicken breast to flatten. Place chive-and-margarine roll at one end of chicken breast and roll up. Secure with toothpick. Dip into milk and roll in bread crumbs. Pour remaining milk and crumbs over chicken. Place in a non-stick baking dish and bake at 350° for 45 minutes. Serves 1.

Note: For additional servings, increase proportions accordingly.

Chicken Supreme

3-4 chicken breasts, skinned and
  cut in half lengthwise
salt and pepper
paprika
garlic salt
2-3 chicken bouillon cubes
1 1/4 cups boiling water
Mushroom Sauce
parsley *or* watercress

Sprinkle chicken with seasonings, and place in a 17" x 11" x 2" baking dish. Combine cubes and water to make broth; pour bouillon over chicken. Cover with foil. Bake at 350° for 1 hour. Uncover and remove any fat. Bake another 45 minutes or until tender. Place chicken on warm platter. Strain pan juices to remove fat. If making ahead, chill until fat rises to top and skim off. Prepare *Mushroom Sauce.*

Mushroom Sauce:
pan juices
1 can mushrooms, drained
2 Tbsp. arrowroot
water

Add pan juices to mushrooms and thicken with arrowroot in small amount of water. Spoon sauce over chicken, and garnish with parsley or watercress. Serves 4-6.

Anne Feltham

French Chicken

1 fryer, skinned and cut up
low-calorie French dressing

Lay chicken pieces in a non-stick pan, and brush with dressing. Bake at 375° for 45 minutes to 1 hour. Great on outdoor grill.

Note: You may skin after cooking also.

Judy Thornton

Fruited Chicken Breasts
(Microwaved)

1/4 tsp. finely grated orange peel
1/2 cup orange juice
1 Tbsp. sliced green onion
1 tsp. chicken bouillon granules
3 medium chicken breasts, skinned
  and split
salt and pepper
paprika
1/2 cup seedless grapes
1 tsp. cornstarch
1 Tbsp. cold water
orange slices

In a 12" x 7" x 2" glass baking dish, combine orange peel, juice, onion, and bouillon. Add chicken; sprinkle with a little salt, pepper, and paprika. Cover dish with waxed paper. Micro-cook for 12 minutes, rearranging after 6 minutes. Place chicken on a warm platter and keep warm. Measure pan juices. Add water if necessary to measure 3/4 cup. Blend corn-starch with cold water; stir into juices. Microcook 2 minutes or until thick, stirring after 1 minute. Add grapes; cook 30 seconds. Spoon sauce over chicken and keep hot. Garnish with orange slices. Serves 6.

Chinese Chicken Barbecue

1 broiler or fryer, cut up
1 chicken bouillon cube
1 cup hot water
1 cup wine vinegar
1/4 cup lemon juice
1/4 cup soy sauce
1/4 cup sweetener

Dissolve bouillon cube in hot water. Add to roasting pan with vinegar, lemon juice, soy sauce, and sweetener. Marinate chicken for 1 hour; turn and marinate another hour. Broil on grill until chicken is well done.

Citrus Chicken

1 chicken, cut up
1 cup orange juice
1 tsp. paprika
1/2 tsp. curry powder
1 tsp. dry mustard

Marinate chicken in juice and seasonings for 1 hour. Cook over coals.

Mandarin Chicken

4 whole chicken breasts, skinned
salt and pepper to taste
dash of paprika
1 can pineapple tidbits, drained
reserved pineapple juice
1 small can mandarin oranges, drained
reserved mandarin orange juice
2 Tbsp. soy sauce
1 1/2 tsp. lemon juice
sweetener to equal 2 Tbsp. sugar
2 tsp. cornstarch or arrowroot
2 Tbsp. raisins
1 small can water chestnuts, diced

Sprinkle chicken breasts with salt, pepper, and paprika. Bake at 350° for 1/2 hour in a shallow baking dish. Meanwhile, make fruit sauce by combining pineapple and orange juices; heat in saucepan, and add soy sauce, lemon juice, and sweetener. Gradually thicken with cornstarch or arrowroot. Add fruit, raisins, and water chestnuts. Pour sauce over chicken and continue baking for 45 minutes or until tender.

Marinated Chicken Breasts

1 1/4 lbs. raw chicken breasts
1/2 cup soy sauce
1/4 tsp. garlic powder
1/2 cup water

Slice chicken breasts across grain of meat in thin slices. Marinate chicken in soy sauce, garlic powder, and water for 8 hours in a glass baking dish. Bake in the marinade at 325° for 1 1/2 hours, turning frequently.

Orange Chicken

1/2 cup soy sauce
8 oz. sugar-free citrus soda
1 cup water
2 chicken bouillon cubes
1/2 tsp. curry powder
1/2 tsp. poultry seasoning or sage
1 chicken, skinned and cut up

Bring all ingredients to a boil, and add chicken. Partially cover and cook on medium heat for 20 minutes. Uncover and continue cooking. Liquid will be a thick sauce. Turn chicken over; marinate on all sides in sauce for 15-20 minutes or until tender.

Oriental Chicken #1

1 chicken, skinned and halved

Marinade:
1 cup orange juice
8 drops sweetener
1 Tbsp. soy sauce
1 tsp. onion powder
1 tsp. dried parsley
1/2 cup pineapple juice
1 tsp. ginger

1/2 cup chopped celery
1/2 cup chopped green pepper
1 cup mushrooms
1 can bean sprouts, drained
orange slices

In a shallow casserole, place chicken and marinade ingredients; refrigerate for 8 hours or overnight. Sprinkle celery, green pepper, and mushrooms over chicken. Bake at 350° for 1 hour. Serve over hot bean sprouts and garnish with orange slices.

Oriental Chicken #2

2 chicken breasts, skinned
1 small can chunk pineapple
1/2 Tbsp. soy sauce
1 tsp. butter flavoring

1 tsp. sweetener
1/4 cup mushrooms
1/2 cup cauliflower
1/4 cup green peppers
2 stalks celery, chopped
1/4 cup chopped onion
2 carrots, sliced
1 Tbsp. cornstarch *or* arrowroot

Simmer chicken breasts in first 4 ingredients until done, either in a pan on top of stove, in a crock pot, or in an oven casserole. Add vegetables and cook until tender-crisp. Remove chicken and vegetables. Add cornstarch or arrowroot to liquid to thicken. Add vegetables and chicken to sauce and serve.

Note: Adjust amounts of vegetables as desired.

Tangy Oven-Fried Chicken

2 chickens, cut up and skinned
1 tsp. salt
1 clove garlic
1/2 cup boiling water
1 tsp. dry mustard
1 Tbsp. water
2 tsp. Worcestershire sauce
1 tsp. oregano
1/8 tsp. Tabasco sauce
1/2 tsp. paprika

Place chicken in a shallow baking pan. Mix remaining ingredients. Baste chicken with mixture. Bake at 350° for 60 minutes. Baste often until tender. Before serving, bake at 400° for 10 minutes or under broiler.

Hazel Marshall

Tavern Chicken–Brunswick Style

1 roaster, skin removed
low-calorie Italian dressing
1 large can peeled tomatoes
1 bay leaf
1 tsp. salt
2 drops sweetener
1 pkg. frozen mixed vegetables
1 pkg. frozen string beans
1 pkg. frozen broccoli pieces
1 1/2 Tbsp. arrowroot

Place chicken in a non-stick baking dish. Brush lightly with dressing. Bake at 350° for 1 hour until tender, but not falling apart. In a large saucepan, combine tomatoes, bay leaf, salt, sweetener, and 2 Tbsp. dressing. Simmer 10 minutes. Add mixed vegetables, string beans, and broccoli. Bring to a boil, cover, and simmer for 15 minutes. Stir in arrowroot to thicken. Place in casserole dish with chicken and bake at 375° for 10 minutes.

Chicken in a Pot

2 carrots, sliced
2 onions, sliced
2 celery stalks, cut in 1" pieces
1 3-lb. chicken with skin, whole *or* cut up
2 tsp. salt
1/2 tsp. coarse black pepper
1/2 cup water, chicken broth, *or* bouillon
1/2 tsp. basil

Put carrots, onions, and celery in bottom of slow cooker. Add whole or cut-up chicken. Top with salt, pepper, and liquid. Sprinkle basil on top. Cover and cook low for 7-10 hours; on high for 2 1/2-3 1/2 hours, using 1 extra cup water.

Glazed Chicken with Carrot Stuffing

1 whole chicken
dash of garlic powder
dash of paprika
pinch of dried parsley
sugar-free orange soda
Stuffing:
4 stalks celery, cut up
6 carrots, shredded
1/2 tsp. butter flavoring
1 oz. orange juice
8 drops sweetener
1/2 tsp. salt
dash of pepper

Sprinkle chicken inside and out with garlic powder, paprika, and parsley. Let stand 3 hours in refrigerator. For *Stuffing*, combine all ingredients. Stuff cavities of chicken. Place chicken breast side up in roasting pan; baste with orange soda and add 8 oz. to pan. Roast at 350°, basting every half hour.

Variation: Use turkey instead of chicken.

Quick Shake Chicken Coating Mix

2/3 cup instant milk powder
1 tsp. salt
1/2 tsp. pepper
1/2 tsp. dry mustard
2 tsp. chicken bouillon

2 tsp. paprika
1 tsp. poultry seasoning

Combine ingredients in plastic bag and drop chicken pieces in, shaking to coat. Place on a non-stick baking pan and bake at 350° for 1 hour or until done.

POULTRY: TURKEY

Turkey à la King

1 Tbsp. vegetable oil
1 large green pepper, diced
1 Tbsp. flour
1 tsp. salt
1 1/2 cups skim milk
3 cups cooked, diced turkey
2 cans mushrooms, drained
1 jar pimientos, drained and diced
1 chicken bouillon cube

In a skillet over medium heat, cook green pepper in oil until tender. Stir in flour and salt. Gradually stir in milk and cook, stirring constantly until thick. Add other ingredients and heat through, stirring often. Reduce heat and simmer 5 minutes. Great over mashed, cooked cauliflower or biscuits, one per person. Serves 6.

Variation: Use chicken instead of turkey.

Note: Freezes well.

Turkey and Stir Fried Spinach

1 Tbsp. vegetable oil
1 clove garlic, crushed
1/4 lb. turkey ham, diced
2 lbs. fresh spinach, washed and trimmed
1/2 tsp. salt
1 tsp. soy sauce
dash of pepper

Heat oil in a large skillet. Add garlic and turkey ham; stir fry to brown lightly. Cut spinach into 3" lengths. Add to skillet and stir fry 1 minute until just wilted. Add salt, soy sauce, and pepper. Stir to mix. Serve immediately. Serves 4.

Turkey Fricassee

1 Tbsp. margarine
1 large green pepper, chopped
2 Tbsp. flour
1 tsp. salt
2 cups skim milk
4 cups cooked, cubed turkey
2 4 1/2-oz. jars mushrooms
1 4-oz. jar pimientos, drained and diced
1 envelope chicken bouillon

In a skillet, simmer green pepper in margarine until tender. Stir in flour and salt until blended. Gradually stir in milk and cook, stirring until thickened. Add turkey, mushrooms, pimientos, and bouillon. Heat to boiling; stir. Reduce to low, cover, and simmer 5 minutes. Spoon over toast, mashed cauliflower, or 1/2 cup cooked brown rice.

Turkey with Chinese Vegetables

2 tsp. cornstarch
2 Tbsp. water
1/4 tsp. sweetener
2 Tbsp. soy sauce
1/8 tsp. salt
pepper
2 Tbsp. oil
3 slices fresh ginger, minced
1/2 cup chicken broth
1 cup shredded Chinese cabbage
1/2 cup bamboo shoots
1/2 cup mushrooms
1/4 cup diced celery
1/4 cup sliced water chestnuts
1/2 cup frozen peas
2 cups diced turkey

Blend cornstarch, water, sweetener, soy sauce, salt, and pepper to make a paste. Heat 1/2 the oil; add ginger and stir fry a few minutes. Add broth and all vegetables, except peas; bring to a boil. Cover and cook 2 minutes. Add peas and turkey; stir briskly. Add cornstarch paste to thicken.

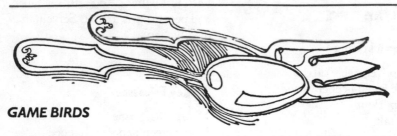

GAME BIRDS

Cornish Hens

Cornish hens, halved*
1 medium onion, sliced
dash of each:
   garlic powder
   pepper
   celery salt
   paprika
*1/2 hen, per serving

Split hens in half. Place onion slices in bottom of pan. Place pieces with skin side up in pan. Sprinkle with remaining ingredients. Cover pan tightly with foil. Bake at 350° for 1 hour. Remove foil and baste hens. Bake 15 minutes longer.

Spiced Cornish Hen

Cornish hen, halved*
1 large onion, thinly sliced
3/4 cup unsweetened pineapple juice
1/4 cup vinegar
1/4 cup soy sauce
1/2 tsp. cinnamon
1/2 tsp. nutmeg
paprika, *optional*

*1/2 hen, per serving

Arrange onion in bottom of a non-stick pan. Place hen halves on top with skin side up. Combine liquids and spices; pour over fowl. Bake at 350° for 50-60 minutes, basting frequently with the pineapple liquid. Sprinkle with paprika for color.

TIPS FOR COOKING WITH FISH
From North Atlantic Seafood Council

Frozen fish might well be called "nature's convenience food." From freezer to table, many fish take less than 30 minutes' preparation time. Defrosting is not necessary before cooking unless you plan to deep fry or sauté. But frying and sautéing do add extra calories. Here are some other ideas for you:

Baking
Preheat oven to 450°. Brush fish with 1 tsp. oil. Place in non-stick pan and season. Bake until fish flakes.

Broiling
Spray broiler pan with Pam. Brush fish with 1 tsp. oil. Broil 2"-4" from heat and season halfway through cooking. Turn.

Steaming
Preheat oven to 450°. Place fish on sprayed foil. Season and wrap securely. Place in shallow baking pan and bake in center of oven.

Poaching in water or bouillon
Place fish on rack in skillet. Pour in seasoned liquid and bring it to a boil. Cover and simmer.

Soup and chowder preparation
Simmer liquids, vegetables, and seasonings long enough to blend flavors and until vegetables are tender, about 30 minutes. Allow a 1-lb. block of frozen fish to stand at room temperature for 15-20 minutes; then cut into 1" cubes and add to other ingredients. Simmer 6-8 minutes until fish is done.

Test for doneness
Fish is cooked when flesh becomes opaque and flakes easily when tested with a fork.

Measure fish at the thickest part
Allow 10-12 minutes cooking time per inch thickness with fresh or defrosted fish. Allow 20-24 minutes cooking time per inch thickness for frozen fish. Bake or oven-steam at 450°.

SEAFOOD: *SPECIFIC CATCHES*

Peachy Cod Bake

1 lb. cod fillets
salt and pepper to taste
1 8-oz. can sliced peaches
1 tsp. margarine
1 tsp. fresh lemon juice
dash of mace
dash of ginger

Thaw fillets if frozen. Season with salt and pepper; arrange in a 2-qt. baking dish. Drain peaches, reserving liquid. Arrange peach slices on top of fish. Combine peach juice, lemon juice, mace, and ginger. Pour sauce over fish and bake in 350° oven for 25 minutes.

Swedish Cod Fish (*Lute Fisk*)

6 oz. cod fish
2 cups boiling water
1/2 cup skim milk
1 tsp. whole allspice
salt and pepper to taste
2 cups cooking liquid
1 tsp. onion flakes
1/2 tsp. butter flavoring
3 tsp. arrowroot

Place cod in boiling water, and boil about 10 minutes until tender. Drain, reserving liquid; fork cod into flakes. In saucepan, combine remaining ingredients, except arrowroot. Thicken with arrowroot mixed in 1 Tbsp. water. Add fish and cook until heated through.

Note: This is a traditional Swedish holiday dish.

Maureen Anderson

Creole Flounder

2 lbs. flounder *or* firm fish fillets
1 1/2 cups chopped tomatoes
1/2 cup chopped green pepper
1/3 cup lemon juice
1 Tbsp. salad oil
green pepper rings
1 tsp. salt
2 tsp. minced onion
1 tsp. basil
1/4 tsp. black pepper
4 drops red pepper sauce

Heat oven to 500°. Place fillets in single layer in baking dish. Stir together remaining ingredients, except pepper rings; spoon over fillets. Bake 5-8 minutes or until fish flakes easily with a fork. Place on warm platter. Garnish with pepper rings. Serves 4-6.

Mediterranean Flounder

1 Tbsp. oil
1 green pepper, cut into 1/2" strips
1 small onion, chopped
1 garlic clove, minced
1 1 1/2-lb. eggplant, cut in 1/2" strips
1 8-oz. can tomato juice
1 Tbsp. margarine
1 Tbsp. lemon juice
1/2 tsp. salt
dash of pepper
1 lb. frozen flounder fillets

Heat oil in a skillet over medium

heat; cook pepper, onion, and garlic about 5 minutes until tender. Add eggplant and tomato juice. Reduce to low heat, cover, and simmer 15 minutes. Meanwhile, heat margarine, lemon juice, salt, and pepper in another pan. Cut frozen flounder fillets crosswise into 4 pieces; place on rack in broiling pan. Baste fillets with lemon-butter sauce. Broil 10-15 minutes, turning once until fish flakes. Serve fish with eggplant sauce. Makes 4 3 1/2-oz. servings after cooking.

Cheryl Doyle

Flounder Provençal

3 4-oz. flounder fillets
butter salt or flavoring
paprika
1/4 cup chopped onion
garlic powder
1 lb. can tomatoes, cut up
1 can chopped mushrooms, drained
1/2 cup water
3 lemon wedges
parsley

Sprinkle each fillet with butter salt and paprika. Roll up fillets; fasten with wooden toothpick. Place in skillet. Add onion and next four ingredients. Cover tightly and simmer about 15 minutes until fish flakes. Remove to warm platter; keep hot. Simmer sauce until a bit thickened and spoon over fish rolls. Garnish with lemon and parsley. Serves 3.

Baked Curried Haddock

1 1/4 lbs. haddock fillets
1 Tbsp. oil
2 onions, finely chopped
1 clove garlic, minced
1 Tbsp. chopped parsley
1/2 cup dry white wine
2 1/2 Tbsp. curry powder
pinch of thyme
pinch of saffron, *optional*
1/2 cup yogurt
salt and pepper
lemon wedges

In oil, sauté onion and garlic until transparent; then spread in a baking dish. Sprinkle with chopped parsley. Place fish fillets on top of vegetables. Combine wine, curry powder, thyme, and saffron; pour over fish. Bake at 400° for 10 minutes. Spread yogurt on top. Sprinkle with salt and pepper; bake 10 minutes more. Garnish with lemon wedges.

Haddock Italiano

1 lb. frozen haddock fillets
1/4 tsp. dried basil
2 Tbsp. chopped onion
1 cup tomato juice
1 can mushrooms, drained
2 oz. shredded Mozzarella cheese

Thaw fish and separate. Place in a glass baking dish. Sprinkle with basil and onion. Cook juice until thickened. Add mushrooms and pour over fish. Bake at 350° for 30 minutes. Top with cheese and return to oven until cheese melts.

Haddock with Vegetables

2 lbs. haddock fillets
1 tsp. salt
1/4 tsp. pepper
1/4 tsp. paprika
3 stalks celery, chopped
6 green onions, chopped
2 carrots, shredded
1 Tbsp. lemon juice

Place fish in an ungreased baking dish. Season with salt, pepper, and paprika. Spread vegetables on fish and sprinkle with lemon juice. Cover and bake 30 minutes or until fish flakes when fork-tested.

Dolores Holowitz

Halibut à l'Orange

3 oranges, peeled and sectioned
1/4 cup sweetener
1/4 tsp. ginger
1 Tbsp. soy sauce
3 lbs. halibut steaks
salt and pepper
1/3 cup brown sugar sweetener
1/3 cup lemon juice
1 Tbsp. dry mustard

Combine orange sections, sweetener, ginger, and soy sauce. Simmer 10 minutes. Sprinkle halibut with salt and pepper; place on a non-stick broiler rack. Combine brown sugar sweetener, lemon juice, and dry mustard. Brush fish steaks with mixture, and broil 4-5 minutes on both sides. Pour warm orange sauce over cooked fish. Serves 6-8.

Halibut with Vegetables

2 lbs. halibut fillets
1 tsp. salt
dash of pepper
dash of paprika
2 carrots, chopped
3 stalks celery, chopped
6 green onions, chopped
1 Tbsp. lemon juice

Place fish in ungreased baking dish. Season with salt, pepper, and paprika. Spread vegetables on fish; season with lemon juice. Cover; bake at 350° 30 minutes or until fish flakes. Serves 6. Try serving with sliced tomatoes and grapefruit sections or orange slices.

Baked Mackerel

10 oz. mackerel
salt and pepper
4 oz. onion, finely sliced
1 1/2 cups vinegar
1 Tbsp. mixed pickling spices

Sprinkle fish with salt and pepper; set in a baking dish. Place onion in the center cavity of fish. Combine vinegar and pickling spices, and pour over fish. Bake at 350° for 30 minutes. Ready when it flakes easily with fork.

Easy Salmon-Potato Escallop

1 small raw potato, peeled and thinly sliced
6 oz. can salmon, drained
1 Tbsp. onion flakes

1/2 cup skim milk
salt and pepper to taste

Alternately layer salmon and potato in small baking dish. Sprinkle each layer with salt, pepper, and onion flakes. Pour milk over all. Bake at 350° until potatoes are tender. Serves 2. Add a salad and a colorful vegetable.

Salmon Loaf with Vegetable Sauce

1 16-oz. can salmon, drained
salmon liquid
skim milk
2 egg whites
1 medium onion, chopped
3 stalks celery, chopped
1 can bean sprouts, drained and
    chopped
2 Tbsp. lemon juice
1 Tbsp. Worcestershire sauce
1/2 tsp. salt
dash of pepper

Skin and flake salmon. Add skim milk to salmon liquid to equal 1 cup. Add other ingredients; mix well. Shape into loaf and turn into a nonstick loaf pan. Bake at 350° for 40 minutes until firm. Let stand 10 minutes before serving. Pass *Vegetable Sauce.*

Vegetable Sauce:
1 pkg. frozen mixed vegetables
1 medium onion, chopped
1 Tbsp. margarine
1 1/2 cups skim milk

2 Tbsp. arrowroot
1 Tbsp. lemon juice
1/4 tsp. dill weed

Sauté vegetables and onion in margarine until tender, about 5 minutes. Add skim milk, thickened with arrowroot. Stir in lemon juice and dill weed. Serve over salmon loaf.

Southern Salmon Bake

1 stalk celery, finely diced
1 green pepper, diced
2 oz. salmon
1 slice toast, crumbed
dash of lemon juice
2 slices pimiento
paprika

Mix celery, green pepper, and fish. Combine with toast crumbs and lemon. Place in a non-stick pan; cover with pimiento slices and paprika. Bake at 350° for 15 minutes. Serve with cucumbers, green beans, or raw cabbage chunks.

Sweet and Sour Salmon

1 7-oz. can salmon
1 Tbsp. white vinegar
1 tsp. sweetener
2 oz. raw onion, finely diced
lettuce
sliced tomatoes

Mix first 4 ingredients together. Serve over lettuce and tomato slices.

Scallops and Mushrooms

8 oz. scallops
paprika
1 tsp. parsley
1 tsp. lemon juice
1 small can mushrooms, drained
1/4 cup tomato juice
pinch of dried basil
dash of garlic powder

Wash scallops well and drain on paper toweling. Sprinkle with paprika, 1/2 tsp. parsley, and 1 tsp. lemon juice. Add mushrooms. Bring tomato juice to a boil in a non-stick pan; then add scallops and simmer for 10 minutes or until scallops are fork tender. Add basil, garlic powder, and remaining parsley. Cook slowly until scallops are soft.

Polynesian Shrimp

8 oz. cooked, deveined shrimp
garlic powder
4 oz. sliced onion, separated into
  rings
2 stalks Chinese cabbage, cut
  diagonally
1 green pepper, cut in strips
1/2 cup pineapple juice
2 Tbsp. vinegar
1 Tbsp. soy sauce
1/2 cup water
1/4 cup drained pineapple chunks

Lightly sprinkle shrimp with garlic. In a non-stick fry pan, cook onion until tender. Add cabbage and green pepper; cook 5 minutes until tender-crisp. Add shrimp. In another saucepan, combine pineapple juice, vinegar, soy sauce, and water; heat, adding pineapple chunks. Cook until hot; then pour over shrimp. Mix well and serve. Serves 2.

Shrimp and Rice Dinner

1/3 cup dry rice
2 1/3 cup water
dash of salt
1/2 green pepper, diced
1/2 tsp. chicken bouillon granules
6 oz. cooked shrimp
1/2 pimiento, diced
1 4-oz. can mushrooms, undrained
1 bay leaf

Place dry rice, water, salt, green pepper, and bouillon in pan. Bring to a boil; then simmer until most of the water has been absorbed. Add remaining ingredients.

Variation: Using 4 oz. cooked rice; decrease water to 1/3 cup. Combine all ingredients and simmer until all liquid has been absorbed.

Shrimp-Squash Casserole

1 tsp. margarine
4 oz. shrimp, chopped raw
1 pkg. frozen yellow squash, cooked
  and drained
1/2 cup chopped onion
1 clove garlic, chopped
1 Tbsp. chopped parsley
salt and pepper to taste
2 Tbsp. plain bread crumbs

Melt margarine. Sauté shrimp. Add squash, onions, garlic, parsley, salt, and pepper. Cook 1/2 hour. Place in a 1-qt. casserole. Sprinkle bread crumbs on top. Bake uncovered at 350° for 1/2 hour.

Cheryl Doyle

Shrimp on a Skewer

1/3 cup lemon juice
3-4 cloves garlic, minced
1 1/2 tsp. salt
1/2 tsp. paprika
1/4 tsp. pepper
1 lb. raw shrimp, cleaned
2 medium green peppers, cut in wedges
2 medium onions, cut in wedges
12 cherry tomatoes

Combine first 3 ingredients; pour over shrimp and refrigerate at least 2 hours. Drain, reserving marinade. On 6 Pam-sprayed skewers, alternate shrimp, green pepper, and onions. Brush with marinade. Broil 3" from heat about 13 minutes, turning once and brushing often with marinade. During last 2 or 3 minutes, place tomatoes on skewers. Serves 4.

Cheryl Doyle

Poached Trout

4 green onions
1/2 cup water
1 large clove garlic, crushed
1 1/2 tsp. salt
1 tsp. Worcestershire sauce
4 small trout fillets
1 large lemon, thinly sliced

In skillet over high heat, cook onions, water, garlic, salt, and Worcestershire to boiling. Add trout and heat through. Reduce to low heat; cover and simmer 8 to 10 minutes until fish flakes; then carefully place fish on a warm platter. Pour pan liquid over fish. Garnish with lemon slices and another chopped green onion. Serves 4.

Cheryl Doyle

Sweet and Sour Snapper

2 8-oz. red snapper fillets
1 tsp. salt
3/4 tsp. pepper
2 Tbsp. chopped onion
2 oz. garlic, minced
1/8 cup water
1/4 cup vinegar
1 Tbsp. ginger root *or* 1 tsp. powdered ginger
sweetener equal to 2 Tbsp. sugar
1/4 medium green pepper, cut into strips
1/4 medium red pepper, cut into strips

Sprinkle salt and pepper on fish. Broil on rack approximately 4" from heat for 5 minutes or until fish flakes easily with fork. Set aside and keep warm. In a non-stick skillet, cook onions, garlic, and water over medium heat 3 minutes or until onion is tender-crisp. Add vinegar, ginger, sweetener, and peppers. Cook 5 minutes or until peppers are tender-crisp. Add cooked fish. Cook another 2 minutes or until thoroughly heated.

Red Snapper with Stuffing

1 lb. red snapper, cleaned and boned
pepper
1/2 cup chicken bouillon
1 tsp. lemon juice
parsley
crushed garlic clove

Season fish inside and out with pepper. Make 3-4 gashes with knife in back of fish to prevent splitting. Place in baking dish. Mix other ingredients and pour over fish. Bake at 400° for 25 minutes until fish flakes but is still moist. Serve with *Stuffing*. Serves 3-4.

Stuffing:
1/2 cup diced celery
2 Tbsp. onion flakes
1 cup minced fresh mushrooms
1 Tbsp. chopped parsley
1/2 tsp. rubbed sage
1/2 tsp. imitation butter flavoring
2 slices bread, crumbed
1/2 cup chicken bouillon

Cover celery and onion flakes with water in a pan and cook until tender. Drain and combine with other ingredients. If too dry, add water to moisten. Turn into a Pam-sprayed pan and bake at 375° for 20 minutes. Spoon over fish.

Sole Roll

1 lb. sole fillets
2 slices bread, crumbed
1/4 cup chopped onion
1 large can mushrooms
1/2 cup chopped parsley
1 Tbsp. lemon juice
1/4 tsp. salt
1 pkg. frozen spinach
1/2 green pepper, chopped
1 can bean sprouts, chopped
1 tomato, sliced

Sprinkle fillets with salt. Combine crumbs, onion, mushrooms, parsley, lemon juice, and salt for the stuffing. Place 1/4 cup stuffing on each fillet; then roll up and secure with toothpicks. Set carefully on cookie sheet and bake at 375° for 20 minutes or until fish flakes easily. Meanwhile, cook spinach with green pepper in small, covered pan about 3 minutes. Add bean sprouts to spinach. Spread mixture in bottom of a baking dish. Add fish and tomato slices. Return to oven for 10 minutes. Makes 4 servings.

Baked Tuna Delight

1 1/2 oz. tuna
1 stalk celery, chopped
1/4 green pepper
1 Tbsp. chives
1 tsp. parsley
1 Tbsp. chopped pimiento
1 small can mushrooms, drained
1 egg white
1 tsp. mayonnaise
1/2 tsp. lemon juice
1/2 oz. Swiss cheese
1 slice bread, crumbed
1 tsp. sesame seeds

In Pam-sprayed casserole, combine tuna, celery, green pepper, chives, parsley, pimiento, and mushrooms.

Combine egg white, mayonnaise, and lemon juice; pour over tuna mixture. Crumble Swiss cheese over top; sprinkle with bread crumbs and sesame seeds. Bake at 425° for 15 minutes. Serves 1.

Baked Tuna Strata

4 slices bread
1 can chopped mushrooms
4 oz. drained tuna
onion flakes
2 oz. grated Swiss cheese
2 eggs
1 cup skim milk
parsley
sliced tomatoes

Place bread in a Pam-sprayed baking dish. Layer mushrooms, tuna, cheese, and onion. Beat eggs with milk and pour over mixture. Bake at 350° for 1 hour. Garnish with parsley and tomato slices. Serves 4.

Chili Tuna

4 oz. water-packed tuna
1 Tbsp. chili powder
1 Tbsp. onion flakes
1/2 tsp. garlic powder
1 green pepper, chopped
1 small can mushrooms, drained
2 stalks celery, diced
1/2 cup tomato juice
salt and pepper
1 slice bread, crumbled

Mix all ingredients, except crumbs, together. Place in a 1-qt. casserole. Top with crumbs. Bake at 400° for 30 minutes.

Hawaiian Tuna Bake

4 oz. tuna, drained
1/2 cup finely chopped celery
1 large can mushrooms, drained
4 slices pineapple, cut into tidbits
1 can French-style green beans, drained
1 oz. Swiss cheese, diced
dash of *each:*
   onion powder
   salt and pepper
   garlic powder

Combine all ingredients; place in a non-stick casserole and bake at 350° for 15 minutes.

Gay Ann Cronce

Hot Tuna Casserole

2 oz. tuna
1 stalk celery, chopped
1/4 green pepper
1 Tbsp. chives
1 tsp. parsley
chopped pimiento
1 can mushrooms, drained
1 egg white
1 tsp. mayonnaise
1/2 tsp. lemon juice
1/2 oz. grated Swiss cheese
1 slice bread
sesame seeds

In non-stick casserole, combine tuna, celery, green pepper, chives, parsley, pimiento, and mushrooms. Blend together egg white, mayonnaise, and lemon juice; pour over tuna mixture. Sprinkle Swiss cheese on top. Crumble bread over all. Sprinkle with sesame seeds. Bake at 425° for 15 minutes.

Creamed Tuna Cups

1 slice crustless white bread
1/2 pkg. cauliflower, overcooked
   and drained
1/2 cup water
1/3 cup instant milk powder
1 envelope unflavored gelatin
salt and pepper
1/2 green pepper, finely diced
1 can drained mushrooms
1 can tuna, drained
paprika

Place bread on aluminum foil and roll out, using rolling pin or bottle. Wet hands and pinch corners of bread together to make a cup-shaped dish. Place cup on foil and bake in 350° oven or broil in broiler until toasted. Then put cauliflower and water into a blender; process. Add milk powder and gelatin; process again. Pour mixture into a saucepan; add salt, pepper, green pepper, and mushrooms. Heat sauce, but *do not boil.* Add tuna and heat again. Pour into toasted cups and sprinkle paprika on top.

Variation: Serve with asparagus spears around cups.

Sweet and Sour Tuna

4 Tbsp. pineapple juice
1/4 cup white vinegar
2 Tbsp. sweetener
2 Tbsp. soy sauce
1 Tbsp. dry onions
2 stalks celery, finely cut
1/2 green pepper, thinly sliced
4 slices pineapple, chopped
8 oz. tuna
1 cup cooked rice *or* bean sprouts

Heat pineapple juice, vinegar, sweetener, and soy sauce until bubbly. Add vegetables and simmer 5 minutes. Add pineapple and tuna; heat through. Serve over hot rice or sprouts.

Ruth Mowbray

Tuna and Peas Casserole

1 7-oz. can water-packed tuna,
   drained
1/2 cup water
1/2 cup cooked peas
1/3 cup instant milk powder
1 egg white
2 Tbsp. chopped onion
2 Tbsp. chopped pimiento
2 tsp. Worcestershire sauce
1/2 tsp. seasoned salt

Combine all ingredients and place in a 1-qt. casserole. Bake in 350° oven for 45 minutes.

Tuna-Cabbage Casserole

8 cups shredded cabbage
2 Tbsp. margarine
1 1/2 Tbsp. cornstarch
2 cups skim milk
salt and pepper to taste
1 tsp. dry mustard
1/2 tsp. Worcestershire sauce
dash of hot pepper sauce

1/2 tsp. horseradish
2 oz. tuna, water-packed
1 can chopped mushrooms
2 oz. grated Muenster cheese

Cook cabbage in boiling water just until wilted; drain well. Melt margarine in saucepan. Add cornstarch and milk. Cook, stirring constantly until thick. Add salt, pepper, dry mustard, Worcestershire, hot pepper sauce, and horseradish. Layer 1/2 the cabbage in a casserole dish; top with 1/2 mushrooms, 1/2 tuna, 1/2 of sauce topped with cheese. Make second layer and bake at 350° for 25-30 minutes.

Tuna Croquettes

1 can tuna, drained
1 slice toasted bread, crumbed
dash of parsley flakes
3 oz. skim milk
salt and pepper to taste

Combine all ingredients. Shape into croquettes or patties. Bake at 350° for 2 minutes on a non-stick cookie sheet. Vegetables may be chopped fine and added to mixture.

Tuna Peppers

3 3/4 oz. tuna, drained
dash of each:
   garlic
   oregano
   paprika

1 slice toasted bread, crumbed
2 green peppers, washed and seeded
2 oz. tomato juice
parsley
1 can mushrooms, drained
1 can bean sprouts, drained

Mix together tuna, garlic, oregano, paprika, and crumbs. Stuff peppers with tuna mixture and place in deep baking dish. Add tomato juice; sprinkle peppers with parsley. Bake in 350° oven for 30 minutes. During last 5 minutes of baking, add mushrooms and bean sprouts to sauce.

Tempting Turbot

Sauce:
1 lb. turbot
3/4 cup tomato juice
1/4 tsp. celery seed
1/4 tsp. chili powder
1/4 tsp. paprika
1/2 tsp. salt
1/4 tsp. pepper
1 Tbsp. onion flakes
1 Tbsp. chopped green pepper
1/2 tsp. sweetener
1/2 tsp. horseradish

Place fish in a flat baking dish. Combine sauce ingredients and pour over fish. Bake at 350° for 30 minutes. Reduce heat to 300° and bake an additional 15 minutes.

SEAFOOD: *FISHERMAN'S CHOICE*

Broiled Fish Cakes

12 oz. shrimp, lobster, crabmeat, *or* fish, finely chopped
2 Tbsp. chopped parsley
1 Tbsp. chopped fresh dill *or* dill seed
1/4 tsp. curry
salt and pepper
1 egg white, slightly beaten
2 Tbsp. instant milk powder

Combine all ingredients, except milk powder and egg white. Form mixture into patties. Dip patties into beaten egg white. Coat with dry milk powder. Broil until brown.

Fish Italiano

1 lb. frozen fish of your choice
1/2 cup pizza *or* spaghetti sauce
1 small onion, diced
1/2 green pepper, diced
1 oz. grated Muenster *or* Mozzarella

Bake fish at 450° in a Pam-sprayed pan until fish begins to soften. Turn once and top with sauce and vegetables. Continue baking about 8 minutes or until fish flakes when forked. Top with grated cheese and return to oven until cheese melts. Serves 2.

Marinated Fish Broil

8 oz. fish fillet of your choice
1/2 cup vinegar
2 Tbsp. lemon juice
2 Tbsp. soy sauce
dash of pepper
salt to taste

paprika

Place fish in a glass baking dish. Combine all other ingredients, except paprika, and pour over fish. Marinate for 30 minutes, turning once with a wooden spoon. Remove fish to Pam-sprayed oven dish; sprinkle with paprika and grill 4" from heat for 8 minutes. Turn, brush with marinade, sprinkle with paprika, and grill 7 minutes more or until fish flakes easily with a fork. Serve hot with parsley garnish and lemon wedges.

Orange-Glazed Fish

10 oz. raw fish (cod, haddock, perch)*
1/2 cup slivered water chestnuts
1 tsp. margarine
1/2 cup orange juice
1 Tbsp. cornstarch
1 Tbsp. chopped chives
1/2 orange, sectioned and cut in chunks

*washed

Place fish in bottom of medium-sized casserole. Salt lightly. In fry pan, lightly brown water chestnuts in margarine. Combine juice and cornstarch; add to chestnuts. Cook until thick. Stir in chives and orange pieces. Pour sauce over fish. Bake at 350° for 30 minutes. Serves 2.

Oriental Fish

2 lbs. thick fish steaks
1/4 cup low-cal Italian dressing
3 Tbsp. soy sauce
1/2 tsp. ginger

freshly ground pepper
lemon slices
parsley

Thaw fish, if frozen. Mix dressing, soy sauce, ginger, and pepper. Marinate fish for 15 minutes. Drain marinade and reserve. Spray pan with Pam or use a non-stick pan. Place fish in pan, and bake at 375° until fish flakes with a fork. Baste once with sauce during cooking. Garnish with lemon slices and parsley. Makes 8 4-oz. servings.

Sensational Baked Fish

1 1/2 lbs. frozen haddock, cod, turbot or other delicate fish
2 Tbsp. vegetable oil or melted margarine
1/2 tsp. onion salt
1/4 tsp. basil

Place frozen fish on oven-proof platter. Combine melted margarine with onion salt and basil. Brush on fish. Bake at 450° for 25-35 minutes or until fish flakes easily with a fork.

Zesty Fish Steaks

2 large fish steaks
1/4 cup tarragon vinegar
salt and pepper to taste
1 Tbsp. Worcestershire sauce
1/4 cup tomato juice
paprika
2 oz. grated Swiss cheese

Place fish steaks skin side up in a shallow baking dish. Combine vinegar, salt, pepper, and Worcestershire; pour mixture over steaks. Marinate 2 hours in refrigerator. Turn fish skin side down. Pour tomato juice over top and sprinkle with paprika. Bake at 350° for 20-25 minutes. Spoon marinade over fish and sprinkle with grated cheese. Broil quickly until cheese melts. Serve immediately. *Measure a 4-oz. portion per person.*

EGG AND CHEESE

Quiche Lorraine
(Cheese Pie)

4 slices bread
2 cups skim milk
4 eggs
4 oz. Swiss cheese
1 can mushrooms, drained

Trim crusts from bread. Lightly toast bread and place in Pam-sprayed dish. In blender, whip all other ingredients. Pour over bread and bake at 350° for 45-55 minutes. Delicious served with a spinach, mushroom, and onion salad.

Quiche Florentine

1 pkg. frozen, chopped spinach, thawed
3 oz. Mozzarella cheese
1 egg
1/4 cup skim milk
dash of pepper
dash of nutmeg

Combine all ingredients and pour into an 8" pie pan. Bake at 325° for 25 minutes.

Lillian Connolly

Broccoli Skillet Quiche

1 Tbsp. margarine
1/4 cup chopped onion
1 1/2 cups chopped, raw broccoli
1 tomato, chopped
1/2 cup shredded Mozzarella cheese
1/2 tsp. salt
dash of pepper
8 eggs, beaten

In a non-stick skillet, melt margarine over medium heat. Add onion and cook until tender. Add broccoli, tomato, cheese, salt, and pepper. Pour beaten eggs over mixture; do not stir. Reduce heat to low. Cover and cook 10 minutes, or until quiche is set. Remove from heat and let stand 5 minutes. Cut in wedges to serve. Serves 4-6.

Spinach Quiche

3/4 cup chopped green pepper
3/4 cup chopped onion
1 1/2 cups sliced mushrooms
1 1/2 cups chopped zucchini
1 1/2 tsp. minced garlic
1 tsp. vegetable oil
4 eggs
1/2 cup Ricotta cheese
1 tsp. salt
dash of pepper
10 oz. spinach, chopped and cooked
1 cup crumbled *or* grated Feta *or* Cheddar cheese

Sauté green pepper, onion, mushrooms, zucchini, and garlic in oil until tender-crisp. Cool. Beat eggs with Ricotta cheese, salt, and pepper. Drain spinach thoroughly, squeezing as much moisture out as possible between paper towels and two plates. Add to egg mixture along with sautéed vegetables and cheese. Mix until well blended. Pour spinach mixture into a non-stick 10" pan and spread evenly. Bake at 350° for one hour or until set in center. Cool 10 minutes before cutting. 4 servings.

Barbara Harris

Egg Foo Yung Casserole
(Slim Living) (Microwave style)

1/2 cup sliced green pepper
1/2 cup sliced onion
1/2 cup sliced celery
1/2 cup raw *or* canned mushrooms
1 Tbsp. water
2 Tbsp. soy sauce
1 can bean sprouts, drained
1/2 cup chopped water chestnuts
salt and pepper to taste
6 beaten eggs
parsley
1/2 tsp. catsup, *optional*

In a glass bowl, combine first 5 ingredients. Cover and place in microwave to steam for 3 minutes. Stir in soy sauce, bean sprouts, water chestnuts, salt, pepper, and eggs. Pour into 4 individual-sized glass casseroles. Micro-cook for 3-4 minutes, turning around once. Garnish with parsley and catsup. Serves 4.

Chiles Rellenos Casserole

6 green chiles
2 or 3 oz. grated Jack cheese
3 egg whites

1/2 tsp. baking powder
salt and pepper

Open chiles and sprinkle cheese inside; roll them up and place seam-side down in a non-stick 8" square casserole. Beat egg whites until stiff; add baking powder. Pour over chiles; sprinkle remaining cheese over top. Bake at 350° for 30 minutes or until batter is golden brown and cheese is melted.   *Margot Purdy*

Marilyn's Chiles Rellenos Casserole

4 slices bread
1 Tbsp. margarine
2 cups grated Muenster cheese
1 4-oz. can green chiles, seeded and
   minced
6 eggs
2 cups milk
2 tsp. paprika
1 tsp. salt
1/2 tsp. crumbled oregano
1/2 tsp. pepper
1/4 tsp. garlic powder
1/4 tsp. dry mustard

Trim crusts from bread. Spread one side with margarine, and place buttered side down in 12" x 7" x 2" baking dish. Sprinkle cheese over bread. Sprinkle minced chiles over cheese layer. In bowl, beat eggs. Add milk and all seasonings. Blend well. Pour over cheese. Cover and chill 4 hours or overnight. Bake, uncovered, at 325° for about 50 minutes or until top is browned. Let stand 10 minutes before serving. Serves 6.

Enchilada Casserole #1

6 corn tortillas
3 oz. Jack cheese, grated
1 medium onion, chopped
1-2 cans green chiles, chopped
1 cup low-fat small-curd cottage
   cheese

Soften tortillas by wrapping them in foil and placing in 350° oven for a few minutes. Place 3 tortillas in a shallow casserole. Sprinkle cheese, onions, and chiles on top. Then layer with remaining tortillas and chiles; top with cottage cheese. Bake at 350° for 15-20 minutes. Serves 4.
         Margot Purdy

Enchilada Casserole #2

1 small onion, halved
dash of *each*:
   rosemary
   basil
   garlic
   ground pepper
   seasoned salt
2 cups chopped tomatoes
1 cup chopped bean sprouts
1 cup cooked brown rice
1 oz. cheese, grated
flour tortillas

Sauté 1/2 the onion with seasonings in a non-stick pan. Add chopped tomatoes; set aside. Sauté chopped bean sprouts, remaining onion half, and brown rice. Place tortillas in baking dish. Spread both mixtures and cheese on tortillas. Bake at 350° for 20 minutes.

SAUCES

Quick Catsup

8 oz. tomato sauce
2 Tbsp. wine vinegar
1/2 tsp. cinnamon
1/4 tsp. cloves
dash of cayenne
dash of nutmeg
dash of ginger
salt and pepper to taste
sweetener to taste

Combine all ingredients and chill. Use as desired.

Chili Sauce

14 oz. tomato juice
1 Tbsp. dry onion flakes
1/2 tsp. salt
1/2 cup white vinegar
1 green pepper, minced
1 stalk celery, chopped finely
1/4 tsp. cinnamon
1/4 tsp. celery salt
1/4 tsp. cloves

Cook ingredients together until thickened to desired consistency. Delicious with meats.

Dill-Tarragon Sauce

8 oz. tomato sauce
2 Tbsp. tarragon vinegar
1/2 tsp. dill seed
1/2 tsp. dried basil

Combine all ingredients thoroughly and chill. This is good as a marinade for steaks, kabobs, fresh or cooked vegetables. Should marinate for 1 hour.

Horseradish Sauce

1 apple, peeled
2 Tbsp. white horseradish
1 tsp. liquid sweetener or to taste

Slice apple very thin; cut into small pieces. Blend all ingredients in blender. Refrigerate. Delicious over salad or fish.

Mushroom Sauce

1 bouillon cube
1/4 cup boiling water
1/2 cup milk
1 1/2 tsp. arrowroot
1 tsp. chives
1 tsp. parsley flakes
1 pimiento, chopped
2 oz. mushrooms, drained and chopped

Dissolve bouillon in water. Add milk and arrowroot, stirring constantly. Cook until cream sauce is thickened. Add chives, parsley, pimiento, and mushrooms.

Variation: Serve as soup; thin with a little milk, heat, and serve.

Orange Sauce for Poultry or Fish

2 tsp. cornstarch
1 cup orange juice
sweetener to equal 1 tsp. sugar
1 orange
2 tsp. grated orange peel
1 Tbsp. raisins, optional

Peel and chop orange. In saucepan, combine cornstarch and orange juice. Cook over medium heat, stirring until thick. Stir in remaining ingredients. Serve warm over meat.

Spaghetti Sauce

1 46-oz. can tomato juice
2 bouillon cubes
dash of onion powder
2 tsp. oregano
1 bay leaf
1 tsp. parsley
basil to taste
1/2 tsp. garlic powder

Mix ingredients and simmer until thickened. Remove bay leaf. Serve over well-drained and rinsed bean sprouts.

Variation: Cook the sprouts in the sauce.

Sweet and Sour Sauce

2 cups white vinegar
2 tsp. sweetener
1/4 cup dill seed
1 cup water
2 tsp. salt
1 stalk celery, thinly chopped
2 Tbsp. onion flakes

Combine ingredients and bring to a boil. Pour over thinly sliced cucumbers, raw cauliflower, or French-style green beans. Makes 1/2 gallon.

Tomato Sauce

1 46-oz. can tomato juice
1/2 tsp. minced parsley
1/4 tsp. garlic powder
1/4 tsp. oregano
1/4 tsp. thyme
several grinds black pepper
salt to taste

Place tomato juice in a large, nonstick baking dish. Put in 350° oven or on stove top until thickened. Combine with remaining ingredients. Mix well and chill. Use as desired.

Desserts, Cakes, Cookies, Pies & Candies

Many of us love sweets. One bite and we can't stop! For special occasions, sweets seem less a temptation since we've already come to associate them with celebration. As long as we don't get *lost* in this type of fare, we should feel free to enjoy sweets, even if sparingly. Besides, there are many natural sweets which do have good food value! 1 Corinthians 10:13 says:

... no temptation is irresistible. You can trust God to... show you how to escape temptation's power so that you can bear up patiently against it. (TLB)

When it comes to sweets, keeping as little around as possible may be the best way to avoid the temptation!

POINTERS TO HEALTHFUL EATING

Don't let the label of "low-calorie" on a dessert recipe fool you. The key is moderation and awareness for you and your family.

Fruit, three times a day, makes a fine natural sweet. Dried fruits are generally high in calories, so go lightly on these. Two level tablespoons of raisins make a fruit portion. One-half cup each of applesauce and crushed pineapple equals a fruit portion also.

If instant milk powder is used, 1/2 cup is equal to 1 cup of reconstituted milk. Where cottage cheese is used, remember that 1/2 cup is a protein portion.

In a starch exchange, 6 tablespoons of cornmeal and 6 of oatmeal are equal to a slice of bread. Instead of refined flours and sugars, we recommend oatmeal, cornmeal, some cereals, unbleached flour, fruits, liquid or granulated sugar substitute called *sweetener* in the recipes.

A shorter baking time is an added benefit in these lower-caloried recipes!

FRUIT CART DESSERTS

Applesauce

1/4 cup lemon juice
4 apples, pared, cored, and cut in
  eighths
sweetener to equal 1/4 cup sugar
dash of cinnamon
dash of nutmeg

Put several pieces of apple and juice in blender; process at *blend* until smooth. Carefully push *puree* button, remove cap, and add remaining apples, a few at a time. Add sweetener and spices. Yields 2 cups.

Chunky Applesauce

10 cooking apples, pared and cored
1/2 cup water
juice of 1/2 lemon
1 tsp. cinnamon
1/4 cup brown sugar sweetener
1/2 cup raisins
1/4 cup nuts

Slice prepared apples. Combine all ingredients in a crock pot. Cover and cook on low for 8-10 hours or until fruit is tender.

Variation: Cook slowly in large, covered pot on top of range until apples are tender but retain some shape. Serve hot or cold.

Presto Applesauce

1 lb. apples, pared and cored
1/2 cup sugar-free black cherry soda
cinnamon

Slice prepared apples. Put small amount of apples with soda into blender, processing until smooth. Add cinnamon and serve.

Baked Apple Bonanza

10 Rome apples
cinnamon
8 oz. sugar-free black cherry soda

Core apples and peel a little skin off top of each. Place in a pan. Sprinkle apples with cinnamon and place stem side down in pan. Pour soda on top. Cover pan and cook on top of stove until apples are tender.

Baked Apples on Grill

cooking apples
pineapple slices
sweetener
cinnamon

Core apples and fill with 1/2 slice pineapple per apple. Sprinkle with sweetener and cinnamon. Place each apple on square of double foil and seal tightly. Bake on coals for 3/4-1 hour, turning occasionally.

Dried Apple Ring

apples, pared and cored

Slice apples in rings. Place rings on a lightly greased cookie sheet, or on clear plastic wrap laid out on a cookie sheet. Dry in an electric oven at low temperature or in a cold gas oven with only the pilot light on.

Drying takes 6-9 hours, so this is a good overnight project. The size of the apple slices and your oven temperature are variables with which you will have to experiment. The apples need not be dried to a crisp. Store them in an airtight container. They should last several weeks at room temperature. Great for traveling!

Grilled Banana

1 banana
sweetener
cinnamon

Cut stem from banana. Slit lengthwise through all except bottom skin. Spread gently and sprinkle sweetener and cinnamon on top. Close banana and wrap in foil. Place on grill for 15 minutes. Serves 1 person.

Orange-Rhubarb Compote

1/4 cup low-cal orange syrup
1 Tbsp. sweetener
1 lb. rhubarb, cut in 1" pieces
2 oranges, sectioned

In saucepan, combine syrup, sweetener, and rhubarb. Bring to a boil, reduce heat, and cover. Cook about 5 minutes or until rhubarb is tender. Remove from heat; stir in orange sections and chill.

Frozen Fruits

pineapple chunks
orange sections
grapefruit sections
1/2" banana slices
maraschino cherries

On a flat dish, place pineapple, orange and grapefruit sections, banana pieces, and a few maraschino cherries for color. Insert a toothpick into each piece. Place in freezer until hard. Remove fruit from freezer about 10 minutes before serving.

Fruit Fondue

1 1/2 cups pineapple juice
1/2 cup lemon juice
1/2 tsp. rum flavoring
2 Tbsp. sweetener
6 tsp. arrowroot

Mix all ingredients and heat until thickened. Dip apples, celery, and banana pieces into warm fondue.

Peaches Supreme

1 lb. peaches, skinned and halved
sugar-free orange soda
2 Tbsp. frozen orange concentrate
grated lemon peel
2 egg whites
8 drops sweetener
1/4 tsp. salt
1/4 tsp. vanilla

Cook peaches in soda for 5 minutes. Place peaches in baking dish. Mix juice and peel; spoon over peaches. Beat egg whites until stiff. Add sweetener, salt, and vanilla; spoon over peaches. Bake at 400° for 8-10 minutes.

Fruit Slices

1 navel orange
1 medium grapefruit
parsley *or* lettuce
maraschino cherries

Cross-cut fruit very thin; cut from center of each section through the skin at one point. Twist each section to make a spiral. Arrange on plate with parsley *or* lettuce; add cherries for color.

Fruit Soup

1 lemon, thinly sliced
1 2" cinnamon stick
3 whole cloves
4 fresh pears, pared and cubed
5 cups cold water
1 6-oz. can unsweetened grape juice concentrate
1 Tbsp. cornstarch
sweetener to equal 1/2 cup sugar

In medium casserole, combine all ingredients, except cornstarch and sweetener. Bring to a boil, cover, and simmer over low heat until pears are tender. Remove cinnamon, cloves, and lemon slices. Combine cornstarch with a little water and mix well. Fold into soup. Cook 5 minutes, stirring occasionally. Add sweetener. Serve cold.

Fruity Combos

1 cup sliced strawberries
1 cup blueberries
or
1 cup grapefruit sections
1/2 cup diced cantaloupe
1/2 cup orange sections
or
1 cup raspberries
1/2 cup diced peaches
1/2 cup sliced banana

Serve combined fruits chilled.

Candied Pineapple

1 fresh pineapple, halved lengthwise
1/2 bottle sugar-free black cherry soda

Scoop out pineapple and cut into 1" chunks. Reserve shells. Cook fruit in soda until slightly tender. Refrigerate to chill. To serve, place pineapple in shell, and pour remaining cooking juice over pineapple.

Exotic Pineapple

1 fresh pineapple
2 cups fresh *or* frozen sliced strawberries
1/4 tsp. vanilla extract
1 tsp. rum extract
sweetener to taste

Cut pineapple in half, lengthwise. Remove center section and cut into small pieces. Reserve shells. Add remaining ingredients to pineapple, and mix well. Spoon back into shells. Broil until heated thoroughly. Serve at once.

Grilled Pineapple

pineapple slices
butter flavoring

cinnamon
brown sugar sweetener

Place pineapple slices on aluminum foil. Sprinkle with butter flavoring, cinnamon, and sweetener. Grill, browning slightly on each side.

Pineapple Crisp

1/2 cup canned or fresh pineapple chunks
1/3 cup instant milk powder
4 Tbsp. water
cinnamon
sweetener

Mix 1/2 of milk, water, and pineapple. Pour into small baking dish. Cover with cinnamon, sweetener, and remaining milk powder. Sprinkle with 2 Tbsp. water. Cover and bake at 350° for 25 minutes or until tender.

Pineapple-Rhubarb Compote

2 cups fresh or frozen rhubarb, chopped
1 cup water
2 cups crushed pineapple, drained
1 tsp. cinnamon
1/2 tsp. salt
nutmeg
ginger
sweetener to taste

Cook rhubarb thoroughly in water. Combine with remaining ingredients. Serve hot or cold.

Jo Ann's Raspberry-Peach Cobbler

1 cup biscuit mix
1/3 cup plus 2 Tbsp. granulated sweetener
3 Tbsp. skim milk
2 tsp. margarine, melted
1 Tbsp. cornstarch
dash of salt
3 cups sliced peaches
1 10-oz. pkg. frozen raspberries, thawed

In bowl, combine biscuit mix, 2 Tbsp. sweetener, milk, and margarine; set aside. In saucepan, blend remaining sweetener, cornstarch, and salt. Stir in fruits. Cook and stir until thickened and bubbly. Pour into a 1 1/2-qt. casserole. Drop dough from teaspoon onto hot fruit, making 6 mounds. Bake at 400° until biscuits are done. Makes 6 servings.

Raisins 'N Crunch

1/3 cup crunchy, non-sugared cereal
2 Tbsp. raisins
1 Tbsp. sunflower seeds

In a small dish, mix all ingredients. Serve. Eat slowly with fingers; it goes too fast with a spoon!

Raisins 'N Such

1 apple
2 Tbsp. raisins
6 walnut halves, broken

Cut up apple into small chunks, leaving the skin on. Add raisins and walnuts.

Strawberries on Grill

1 qt. fresh strawberries
sweetener
2 tsp. pineapple juice

Wash and hull berries; slice in a bowl. Sprinkle with sweetener and let stand 1/2 hour. Divide into 1/2 cup servings, and place on squares of foil, doubled. Add 2 tsp. pineapple juice to each and seal well. Place on grill and cook over slow fire 7-8 minutes. Serve warm over cheesecake.

DESSERTS: PUDDINGS

Chocolate Tapioca Pudding

2 eggs, separated
1/2 cup water
2 envelopes low-cal hot cocoa mix
dash of salt
2 Tbsp. tapioca
1 tsp. vanilla
2 Tbsp. raisins
12 walnut meats, chopped

Mix yolks with water. Add cocoa, salt, and tapioca. Bring to boiling point, stirring constantly. Cool and add vanilla. Whip egg whites until stiff. Fold into chocolate mixture. Add raisins and nuts. Place into sherbet dishes and chill. Makes 4-6 servings.

Note: A low-cal hot cocoa mix recipe is in the beverage section.

Impossible Pumpkin Pudding

2 eggs
1 tsp. cinnamon
1/4 tsp. salt
1/4 tsp. cloves
5 pkgs. granulated sweetener
1 can evaporated skim milk and water to equal 2 cups
2 slices bread, crumbed
1 tsp. baking powder

Process all ingredients in blender for 2 minutes at low speed. Pour into a non-stick pan. Bake at 350° for 45-50 minutes.

Variation: If desired, 2/3 cup instant milk powder and enough water to equal 2 cups may be substituted for evaporated milk.

Rena Canull

Raisin Bread Pudding

1 cup skim milk
1 slice bread, cubed
1 egg beaten or egg substitute equivalent
1/2 tsp. vanilla
1/4 tsp. cinnamon
1/4 tsp. nutmeg
sweetener to equal 1/2 cup sugar
1 Tbsp. raisins

In baking dish, combine all ingredients. Set in a pan with water about 1" deep. Bake at 375° for 40 minutes or until set.

Custard with Strawberry Sauce

Custard:
4 eggs
2 cups skim milk

sweetener to taste
1/4 tsp. salt

Sauce:
1 cup fresh strawberries
sweetener, *optional*

Beat custard ingredients together. Place in shallow pan set in larger pan with 1" water in bottom. Bake in 325° oven for 50-55 minutes. Check center of custard with knife to see if set. Remove from oven and cool. Mash fresh strawberries. Add sweetener, if desired. Spoon layer of custard and strawberries into dessert cups. Garnish with extra strawberries.

WHIPPED & CHILLED DESSERTS

Almond Bavarian

1 envelope gelatin
1/4 cup cold water
8 oz. boiling water
1 cup cottage cheese
8 oz. evaporated skim milk
1/3 cup instant milk powder
1 Tbsp. sweetener
1/4 tsp. almond extract

Soften gelatin in cold water; add boiling water to dissolve. Blend together remaining ingredients. When well blended, add to gelatin mixture, and pour into a 1 1/2-qt. mold to set. Chill.

Variation: Fruit may be added.

Cherry Mousse

1 envelope unflavored gelatin
1/2 cup skim milk
1 10-oz. can unsweetened cherries
sweetener to taste
3 egg whites
1/8 tsp. salt
1 cup evaporated skim milk, chilled

Sprinkle gelatin over skim milk in saucepan to soften. Place pan over low heat for 3 minutes, stirring constantly. Remove from heat and stir in cherries. Beat egg whites with salt until stiff, but not dry; then fold into cherry mixture. Whip evaporated milk until stiff; fold into cherry-egg mixture. Pour mixture into a 6-cup mold or a serving bowl, and chill until firm. Makes 8 servings.

Choco-Cola Whip

1 envelope unflavored gelatin
1 cup boiling water
1/3 cup low-cal chocolate milk
   powder
1/4 tsp. vanilla
1 cup sugar-free chocolate soda
sweetener to taste

Dissolve gelatin and chocolate powder in water over low heat. Remove from heat and stir in vanilla, soda, and sweetener. Pour into mixing bowl. Chill to consistency of egg white. Beat until fluffy. Chill again until set. Serves 6.

Note: Use store-bought Alba brand chocolate milk powder.

Joyce Premeaux

Apple Berry Freeze

2 cups applesauce
1 tsp. cherry extract
1 Tbsp. lemon juice
1/2 tsp. lemon rind
5 drops almond extract
1 cup skim milk

Combine all ingredients and mix thoroughly. Pour into ice cube trays. Place in freezer until frozen 1/2" from sides. Pour into a bowl and beat with mixer until fluffy.

Chocolate-Banana Whip

1/2 cup cold water
1 envelope low-cal chocolate milk
  powder
6 ice cubes
1 medium, fully ripe banana
1/4 cup cottage cheese

In blender, combine cold water and chocolate powder. Cover and blend at low speed. Add ice cubes, banana, and cottage cheese. Blend at high speed about 1 minute until smooth and thick. Makes 2 servings.

Choco-Pineapple Delight

1 cup crushed pineapple
2/3 cup low-cal chocolate milk
  powder

Mix fruit and powder together. Place in shallow dish and freeze. When frozen, cut into small chunks and eat frozen.

Lemon Meringue Dessert

2 envelopes unflavored gelatin
24 oz. sugar-free lemon beverage
juice and rind from 1/2 fresh lemon
sweetener to equal 4 tsp. sugar
15 drops yellow food coloring

In large bowl, soften gelatin in beverage. Add lemon juice, rind, sweetener, and food coloring. Refrigerate until firm. When fully hard, put in blender and whip until fluffy. Pour into square pan. Serve with "Meringue Topping," if desired.

"Meringue" Topping

1 envelope unflavored gelatin
12 oz. sugar-free creme soda
1/3 cup instant milk powder
sweetener to equal 2 Tbsp. sugar

Soften gelatin in soda. Add milk powder and sweetener. Set until hard. Whip in blender until fluffy.

Melon Fluff Cooler

2 envelopes unflavored gelatin
1 pkg. sugar-free lemon or orange
  drink mix
sweetener to taste
3/4 cup cold water
1 cup boiling water
1/4 cup orange juice
1 cup melon balls
1/3 instant milk powder

Dissolve gelatin, drink mix, and sweetener, in cold water. Add hot water and orange juice. Divide liquid mixture, allowing half of it to thicken. Fold in melon balls. Pour into serving dish; chill until set, but not firm. Chill remaining mixture to thicken slightly; add milk powder. Set bowl into a bowl of ice water and whip until thick and doubled. Put on top of gelatin with melon balls. Garnish with remaining melon balls. Chill.

Orange Whip

1 envelope dietetic orange gelatin
1 cup boiling water
3/4 cup cold water
1 tsp. freshly grated orange peel
2 Tbsp. granulated sweetener
1 egg white
1 orange, peeled and chopped

Dissolve gelatin in hot water. Add cold water and orange peel. Chill until partially set. Beat egg white to soft peak stage; gradually add sweetener. Continue beating until stiff. Beat thickened gelatin at high speed until foamy and doubled in volume. Continue to beat, slowly adding whipped egg white. Fold in orange pieces. Spoon into a 1-qt. mold and chill. Very low in calories!

Peach-Almondine Glacé

1 can water-packed peaches, drained
1/3 cup skim milk
1/2 tsp. almond extract
2 Tbsp. sweetener
8 oz. cottage cheese
sliced maraschino cherries

Divide peaches among 5 dessert dishes. Combine remaining ingredients in blender until smooth and creamy. Pour over peaches and refrigerate 3 hours. Top each with several maraschino slices for color.

Pineapple Creme Delight

2 envelopes dietetic lemon gelatin
1 cup boiling water
1 8 1/2-oz. can crushed pineapple
6 nuts, chopped
4 Tbsp. instant milk powder
4 Tbsp. ice water
4 drops sweetener
dash of nutmeg

Dissolve gelatin in boiling water. Chill until thickened. Stir in pineapple and nuts. Combine milk, water, sweetener, and nutmeg; beat at high speed until stiff peaks form. Fold whipped topping into gelatin. Spoon into a 4-cup mold and chill 2 hours or until firm. Makes 4-6 servings.

Pear-Whip Delight

1/2 cup sugar-free orange soda
1/2 cup sugar-free lemon-lime soda
2 drops red food coloring
1/2 tsp. coconut extract
1 envelope unflavored gelatin
1/4 cup evaporated skim milk
4 pear halves

In blender, place first 5 ingredients; blend 15 seconds. Add skim milk and blend 20 seconds more. Place pear halves in flat-bottomed dessert dish. Pour soda mixture over pear halves. Chill until set. Serves 2.

Peach and Orange Sherbet

2 1-lb. cans peach slices
sweetener to equal 1/2 cup sugar
1/4 cup water
1/4 cup unsweetened grapefruit juice
1/4 cup unsweetened orange juice
1 Tbsp. lemon juice
2 egg whites

About 6 hours before serving, drain syrup from peach slices. Puree enough peaches to make 1 3/4 cups puree. In medium bowl, mix remaining ingredients, except egg whites. Freeze 30 minutes until firm about 1" from edge of bowl. Then with mixer, beat fruit until smooth. Stiffly beat 2 egg whites, and fold into sherbet mixture. Freeze until just firm and serve immediately. Makes 1 qt. or six 2/3 cup servings.

Peppermint Bavarian

1 envelope unflavored gelatin
1/4 cup cold water
1 1/2 cups skim milk
8 drops sweetener
1/4 tsp. peppermint extract
4 drops red food coloring, *optional*
1/3 cup water
1/3 cup instant milk powder

Soften gelatin in cold water. Heat milk and sweetener, stirring constantly until bubbles form around edge of pan. Add gelatin, extract, and optional food coloring. Chill until slightly thickened. Pour water into small bowl; sprinkle milk powder over surface, and beat until stiff.

Fold into gelatin mixture and spoon into sherbet glasses.

Strawberry Foam

1/2 cup sugar-free strawberry soda
1 pkg. dietetic strawberry gelatin
1 egg white
1 1/2 cups crushed ice

Combine soda and gelatin in blender; process and add egg white and ice.

Note: This is a pudding-like treat which sets up fast, so be sure to take it out of the blender at once.

Strawberry Mousse

1 envelope unflavored gelatin
1/2 cup boiling water
1 cup skim milk
1 cup strawberries

In a large bowl, blend together gelatin and boiling water. Add skim milk and strawberries. Blend for a few seconds. Refrigerate at least one hour before serving.

Strawberry-Apple Whip

1 cup sugar-free applesauce
1 envelope dietetic strawberry gelatin
1 cup evaporated skim milk

Heat applesauce and gelatin together. Add evaporated milk. Chill until partially set. Whip and serve immediately.

Variation: Use 1 cup 99% fat-free condensed milk.

Strawberry Whip

1/2 cup evaporated skim milk
2 cups fresh or frozen strawberries
2 egg whites
3 tsp. sweetener
6 strawberries

Pour skim milk into small pan. Place in freezer 30 minutes until crystals form around edge. Meanwhile, place strawberries in blender; process until smooth. In small bowl, beat egg whites until stiff. Fold strawberry puree into egg whites. Whip chilled mixture until foamy. Add sweetener and continue beating until thick and fluffy. Fold in strawberry mixture. Serve with whole strawberries for garnish.

Strawberry-Pineapple Dessert

1 envelope unflavored gelatin
4 tsp. sweetener
2 tsp. vanilla
1 Tbsp. lemon juice
1 cup pineapple juice
1 1/3 cups instant milk powder
1 can pineapple chunks
1 cup strawberries, unsweetened

Dissolve gelatin in 1/4 cup pineapple juice. Boil another 1/4 cup pineapple juice, and combine with gelatin mixture. Add final 1/2 cup juice. Combine gelatin mixture and milk; beat until stiff, about 10 minutes. Add sweetener, vanilla, and lemon juice. Blend. Fold in fruit and put into an 8" square pan. Refrigerate or freeze.

Three-Fruit Sherbet

1 medium banana
1 16-oz. can crushed pineapple
1/2 6-oz. can frozen orange juice
1/2 cup instant milk powder

Blend ingredients for 30 seconds and freeze.

DESSERTS: YOGURT

Basic Yogurt

1 qt. skim milk
2 Tbsp. instant milk powder
1 Tbsp. commercial yogurt

While stirring, bring both milks to a slow boil. Cool to lukewarm (110°). Add yogurt and blend until smooth, stirring gently. Place in covered bowl; set in a warm place until of creamy consistency. Then refrigerate.

Variation: Place mixture in a wide-mouth thermos; let set until ready.
                                        Gail Bender

Frozen Yogurt Whip

2 6-oz. cartons plain low-fat yogurt
2 cups low-calorie whipped topping
3/4 cup any berries or fruit
sweetener to taste, *optional*

Fold yogurt into topping and fruit of your choice. Add sweetener, if desired. Pour into an 8" square dish. Cover and freeze until firm. Makes 6-8 servings.

Note: Don't use the sugared topping found in the freezer at the store.

Peach Yogurt

1 lb. fresh, frozen, or canned,
  water-packed peaches
1/4 cup water
1 Tbsp. arrowroot
sweetener to taste
1 small container plain yogurt

Place 1/2 lb. peaches and water in blender; process until smooth. Place in saucepan and heat. Add arrowroot dissolved in water; heat until thick. Add sweetener. Drain remaining peaches and chop. Add to sauce and cool. Stir into yogurt and chill.

Note: If using fresh peaches, cook 1/2 quantity in small amount of water until tender; then blend. If using frozen peaches, thaw and add small amount of water before blending 1/2 quantity.

Frozen Yogurt Pops

1 6-oz. carton yogurt
1 wooden stick or plastic spoon
Flavor choices:
3 Tbsp. dietetic strawberry jam or
3 Tbsp. finely chopped peaches or
3 Tbsp. low-cal chocolate milk
  powder or
4 Tbsp. sugar-free applesauce and
  1/2 tsp. cinnamon

Combine yogurt and flavor choice. Divide mixture into two 4-oz. paper cups. Freeze upright about 30 minutes until firm enough to hold wooden stick. Insert wooden stick or plastic spoon into center of each pop. Freeze until firm. To serve, peel off paper cup.

Fruity Yogurt Squares

2 envelopes unflavored gelatin
1/2 cup pineapple juice
16 oz. low-fat plain yogurt
sweetener to taste
1 tsp. vanilla
1/2 cup crushed pineapple
1/2 cup sliced strawberries

Dissolve gelatin in boiling pineapple juice. Add yogurt, sweetener, vanilla, and pineapple. Pour into an 8" square pan. Garnish with strawberries. Chill until firm. Cut into squares.

Variation: Try other fruit combinations.

Pineapple Yogurt Dessert

1 small can crushed pineapple
1 envelope unflavored gelatin
sweetener, optional
2 8-oz. cartons plain yogurt

Drain pineapple juice in pan; stir in gelatin and dissolve. Heat to boiling. Add pineapple and set aside until thick. Add yogurt just before gelatin is completely set. Pour into small mold.

Purple Passion

1 small container low-fat yogurt
1/2 cup frozen unsweetened
  blueberries
sweetener to taste
1 tsp. vanilla
1 Tbsp. orange juice
3/4 lb. frozen, unsweetened mixed
  fruit, finely chopped

Combine all ingredients and place in a 1-qt. mold. Freeze.

Variation: Use one fruit instead of mixed fruit.

Strawberry-Pineapple Yogurt Pudding

1 can crushed pineapple
1 envelope unflavored gelatin
1 Tbsp. sweetener
2 cups plain yogurt
1 cup chopped strawberries

Drain pineapple. In saucepan, combine gelatin and sweetener; stir over low heat until dissolved. Add pineapple. Cool until slightly thick. Fold in yogurt and strawberries. Place in sherbet dishes. Garnish with extra strawberries. Chill at least 2 hours.

Strawberry-Pineapple Yogurt Squares

1/2 cup drained, crushed pineapple
1/2 cup reserved pineapple juice
2 envelopes unflavored gelatin
1 small container low-fat plain
    yogurt
sweetener to taste
1 tsp. vanilla
brown sugar sweetener
1/2 cup thinly sliced strawberries

Heat pineapple juice to boiling. Add gelatin and dissolve. Stir in yogurt, sweetener, and vanilla. Add pineapple. Pour into a small non-stick pan. Sprinkle top with sweetener. Garnish with strawberries. Refrigerate until firm. Cut in squares.

CAKES: *BAKED*

Angel Food Cake

12 egg whites
1 1/2 tsp. cream of tartar
1/4 tsp. salt
1 1/2 tsp. vanilla
30 drops sweetener
1/2 cup instant milk powder
4 slices bread, crumbed

Beat egg whites with cream of tartar, salt, vanilla, and sweetener until soft peaks form, but are still moist and glossy. Add milk powder a little at a time and continue beating until peaks are stiff. Fold in bread crumbs by fourths. Bake in ungreased tube pan at 375° for 30-40 minutes. Cool cake in pan before removing.

Apple-Dapple Chocolate Cake

4 slices toasted bread, crumbed
3 apples
1 tsp. chocolate extract
1 envelope low-cal chocolate milk
    powder
5 tsp. sweetener
1/2 tsp. cinnamon
1/4 cup water
2 egg whites

Place bread crumbs in a bowl. Core apples and chop in blender; combine with remaining ingredients and add to bread crumbs. Mix until well blended. Fold in egg whites. Pour into a non-stick 8" square pan. Bake at 350° for 45 minutes.

Applesauce Cake

1 slice toasted white bread, crumbed
1 tsp. water
1/2 cup applesauce
1/4 tsp. lemon rind
2 drops sweetener
1 Tbsp. sesame seeds

Mix crumbs and water; flatten into small pie pan. Let harden in refrigerator. Combine applesauce, lemon rind, and sweetener. Fill pie pan with mixture and sprinkle with sesame seeds. Chill.

Banana Cream Roll

2 medium eggs
2/3 cup instant milk powder
1 medium banana, sliced
1 slice white bread, shredded
sweetener equal to 4 tsp. sugar
1 1/2 tsp. vanilla extract
1/2 tsp. cream of tartar
1/2 tsp. baking soda

Cream Filling:
2/3 cup cottage cheese
sweetener to equal 4 tsp. sugar
2 tsp. vanilla extract

In blender, combine all non-filling ingredients and process until smooth. Pour mixture into a non-stick 16" x 11" shallow baking pan. Bake at 350° for 10 minutes or until lightly browned. Set aside to cool. In a blender container, combine filling ingredients; process until smooth. With a spatula, remove roll from baking pan and place on a piece of aluminum foil top side down. Spread evenly with filling and roll from narrow end. Cut in half and wrap each half in foil; freeze. Remove from freezer and let stand 2-3 hours before serving. Makes 2 servings.

Banana Cupcakes

4 Tbsp. margarine
1 Tbsp. sweetener
1/3 cup instant milk powder
1 tsp. vanilla
4 slices bread, crumbed
1/4 tsp. salt, *optional*
3 Tbsp. buttermilk
2 bananas, mashed
1/4 cup mushrooms, broiled, chopped
4 egg whites, stiffly beaten
1/3 tsp. cream of tartar

Cream together margarine, sweetener, milk powder, and vanilla. Beat in crumbs and salt. Stir in buttermilk, bananas, and mushrooms. Fold in egg whites and cream of tartar. Pour into an 8-muffin tin. Bake at 350° for 25-30 minutes.

Chocolate Banana Cupcakes

2 medium-sized eggs
1 medium banana, peeled and mashed
1/2 tsp. chocolate extract
1/2 tsp. vanilla
1 slice bread, crumbed
2 envelopes low-cal hot chocolate drink mix
4 tsp. sweetener
1/2 tsp. baking powder

Beat eggs. Add banana and extracts.

In separate bowl, combine remaining ingredients. Fold in egg mixture. Pour batter into a non-stick muffin tin. Bake at 350° for 15-20 minutes. Makes 8 cupcakes.

Pineapple-Carrot Cake

4 slices toasted bread, crumbed
2/3 cup instant milk powder
3 envelopes sweetener
2 grated carrots
1 cup unsweetened crushed
  pineapple, drained
4 eggs
1 Tbsp. vanilla
2 tsp. cinnamon
1/2 tsp. ginger

Combine crumbs, milk powder, and sweetener. Add grated carrots and pineapple. Beat eggs for 5 minutes; add vanilla, cinnamon, and ginger. Add egg mixture to dry ingredients. Mix well. Put into a non-stick muffin tin or baking dish. Bake at 350° for 20 minutes.

Holiday Fruit Cake

1 1/3 cups instant milk powder
6 Tbsp. pineapple juice
30 drops sweetener
1/2 cup orange juice
2 Tbsp. lemon juice
2 apples, grated with peel
6 slices pineapple, chopped
2 cups chopped cranberries
2 tsp. cinnamon
2 tsp. vanilla
8 slices toasted bread, crumbed

Combine milk powder, pineapple juice, sweetener, orange juice, and lemon juice. Mix with beater until stiff. Add apples, pineapple, and cranberries; mix well. Add cinnamon and vanilla. Fold in bread crumbs. Pour into a non-stick 8" square pan. Bake at 250° for 1 1/2 hours.

Pineapple Upside-Down Cake

8 slices pineapple
1 cup pineapple juice
3 tsp. sweetener
1 tsp. cinnamon
1 tsp. vanilla
1 tsp. coconut flavoring
1 1/3 cups instant milk powder
2 tsp. sweetener
pinch of cinnamon
2 envelopes unflavored gelatin
1/2 cup cold water
1/2 cup hot water

Simmer first 6 ingredients together, for 10 minutes. Mix together milk powder, sweetener, and cinnamon; set mixture aside. Dissolve gelatin in cold water; then add hot water. Pour over pineapple mixture and place in a 9" pie tin. Sprinkle milk mixture over pineapple. Sprinkle water on top to keep moist. Press with spoon. Bake at 350° for 20 minutes; then refrigerate until gelatin sets up.

Devil's Food Cake

1 slice bread, crumbed
1 medium egg, lightly beaten
1/4 cup plain yogurt
sweetener to equal 8 tsp. sugar
1 envelope sugar-free hot chocolate
    drink mix
1 tsp. vanilla
1/2 tsp. baking soda
23 drops red food coloring, *optional*

In medium bowl, blend all ingredients thoroughly by hand. Pour batter into a 5" x 3" non-stick loaf pan or divide among 5 medium, non-stick cupcake tins. Bake loaf at 350° for 20-25 minutes; cupcakes for 15-20 minutes or until toothpick inserted into middle comes out clean.

Chocolate Cake

4 slices white bread, crumbed
2/3 cup instant milk powder
4 eggs
1 Tbsp. vanilla
1 Tbsp. chocolate extract
brown food coloring
sweetener to equal 12 Tbsp. sugar

Combine bread and milk powder. Mix well. In mixing bowl, beat eggs 5 minutes at medium speed. Add extracts and coloring. Beat 5 minutes. Stir egg mixture into dry ingredients. Mix well. Pour into a wax paper-lined, 8" square pan. Bake at 350° for 30 minutes.

CAKES: ICE-BOX CAKES

Light 'N Lemony Cheesecake

2 envelopes gelatin
1/2 cup cold skim milk
1 cup boiling milk
2 Tbsp. liquid sweetener
2 Tbsp. lemon rind
3 Tbsp. lemon juice
1 tsp. vanilla
1/4 tsp. salt
16 oz. cottage cheese
2 egg whites
1 can crushed pineapple
4 slices toasted bread, crumbed

Spread crumbs into bottom of a 9" pie tin; set aside. Sprinkle gelatin over cold milk in blender; allow to soften. Add boiling milk, cover, and process 35-60 seconds until gelatin dissolves. Add sweetener, lemon rind, lemon juice, vanilla, and salt. Cover and blend at high speed for 1 minute. Add cottage cheese 1 cup at a time, blending after each addition. Pour into large bowl. Cover and refrigerate 30 minutes, stirring occasionally until mixture mounds lightly when dropped by a spoon. Beat egg whites until stiff and fold into gelatin mixture. Fold in drained pineapple. Pour into pie crust.

Slim Line Cheesecake

3 envelopes unflavored gelatin
1/2 cup cold water
1 qt. buttermilk
2 tsp. vanilla
5 tsp. sweetener

1/4 tsp. yellow food coloring
1/2 cup pineapple, blueberries, or
    strawberries

In a 2-qt. saucepan, sprinkle gelatin on cold water. Heat, stirring to dissolve (don't overheat); remove from heat. Add buttermilk, vanilla, sweetener, and food coloring. Blend. Pour into an 8" square cake pan and refrigerate. When chilled, add fruit to top.

Stained Glass Cake

1 envelope dietetic orange gelatin
1 envelope dietetic cherry gelatin
1 envelope dietetic lime gelatin
4 cups boiling water
1 1/2 cups cold water
1 envelope dietetic lemon gelatin
granulated sweetener to equal
    1/4 cup sugar
1/2 cup canned pineapple juice
1 8-oz. can evaporated milk, chilled

Prepare orange, cherry, and lime gelatins separately, using 1 cup boiling water and 1/2 cup cold water for each. Pour each flavor into a separate 8" square pan. Chill until firm about 3 hours or overnight. Cut into 1/2" cubes. Set aside a few of each to garnish. Dissolve lemon gelatin and sweetener in 1 cup boiling water. Stir in pineapple juice. Chill until slightly thickened. Whip chilled milk until firm peaks form. Blend into slightly thickened lemon gelatin. Fold in gelatin cubes. Spoon into a 9" spring-form pan. Chill until

firm, at least 5 hours or overnight. Just before serving, run a spatula around sides of pan; then gently remove. Garnish top with reserved gelatin cubes. Serves 16.

COOKIES AND BARS

Apple-Nut Cookies

2 medium apples, pared, cored, and
    grated
sweetener to taste
2/3 cup instant milk powder
1/2 tsp. cinnamon
dash of nutmeg
dash of ginger
1/8 tsp. vanilla
1/4 tsp. butter pecan flavoring

Combine all ingredients and drop onto non-stick cookie sheet. Bake on top shelf of oven at 350° for 15 minutes.

Applesauce Cookies

1 cup sugar-free applesauce
1 1/3 cups instant milk powder
1 tsp. vanilla
sweetener to taste
12 nuts
1/4 cup raisins
1/2 tsp. cinnamon

Combine all ingredients together. Drop by teaspoonfuls onto a non-stick cookie sheet. Bake at 375° for 10-15 minutes.

Apple Thins

1 apple, cored
4 oz. cooked pumpkin
1 Tbsp. liquid sweetener
1/2 tsp. cinnamon
1/4 tsp. nutmeg
2/3 cup milk powder
1/2 tsp. almond extract
cinnamon

Grate apple; add remaining ingredients. Drop by teaspoonfuls onto baking sheet; flatten each with a spoon. Bake at 375° for 20 minutes. Remove from oven. Sprinkle with cinnamon. Serve warm.

Chocolate-Apple Cookies

2 baking apples, pared and grated
4 tsp. granulated sweetener
2/3 cup low-cal chocolate milk powder

Combine all ingredients in mixing bowl. Drop by teaspoonfuls onto non-stick cookie sheet. For crunchier cookie, flatten slightly before baking. Put in a non-preheated oven; then, heat to 350° and bake approximately 40 minutes. When edges of cookies begin to brown, cookies are done. Remove immediately from sheet. Makes approximately 18 cookies.

Crunchy Cinnamon Cookies

1 slice toasted bread, crumbed
1/8 tsp. cinnamon
1/8 tsp. nutmeg
3 drops sweetener
2 tsp. cold water

Mix all ingredients together with hand to form a stiff dough. Then form into six small balls. Place on aluminum foil and flatten with palm. Place foil on cookie sheet. The flatter the cookie, the crispier it will be. Bake at 300° for 12 minutes. Turn cookies and bake another 3 minutes until brown.

Oatmeal Cookies

2 egg whites, beaten stiff
20 drops sweetener
1/4 tsp. cream of tartar
1/4 tsp. cinnamon
1/4 tsp. nutmeg
1/2 cup oats
1/3 cup instant milk powder

Mix all ingredients together. Drop by teaspoonfuls onto a non-stick cookie sheet. Bake at 275° for 15-20 minutes until edged in brown. Makes 16 small cookies.

Pumpkin Cookies

4 oz. pumpkin
3 tsp. sweetener
1 tsp. cinnamon
1/4 tsp. ginger
1/2 tsp. maple flavoring
1/3 cup instant milk powder

Mix all ingredients together and drop by teaspoonfuls onto non-stick pan. Bake at 450° for 25 minutes.

Variation: Add 1 Tbsp. raisins and 6 walnut halves.

Note: For bar cookies, double recipe.

Pineapple Cookies

1 cup drained, crushed pineapple
1 1/3 cups instant milk powder
1/2 tsp. vanilla
1-2 tsp. sweetener

Mix all ingredients together and drop by teaspoonfuls onto non-stick cookie sheet. Bake at 350° for 15-20 minutes, until edge is brown. Remove while hot.

Variation: Add different food colorings and extracts.

Chocolate Brownies

2 eggs, separated
1/4 cup water
1/2 tsp. baking powder
1/4 tsp. maple extract
sweetener to equal 2 tsp. sugar
2 slices bread, crumbed
2 envelopes low-cal chocolate milk powder

Beat egg yolks with water. Add baking powder, extract, sweetener, bread crumbs, and chocolate powder. Mix well. Beat egg whites until stiff, but not dry. Fold into chocolate mixture. Pour into an 8" non-stick pan. Bake at 350° for 10-12 minutes. Cool. Cut into bars. Makes 16.
Betty Butler

Chocolate-Peanut Butter Treats

2/3 cup low-cal chocolate milk powder
1/2 cup oatmeal
2 Tbsp. peanut butter
1 tsp. vanilla
1/2 tsp. cinnamon
1 cup sugar-free applesauce
12 walnut halves
2 Tbsp. raisins

Blend all ingredients together well; put into a Pam-sprayed 8" square pan. Bake at 350° for 15-30 minutes, depending on how soft you want them.

Variation: Add 1/4 tsp. nutmeg and 4 tsp. brown sugar sweetener.

Crunchy Bars

2 egg whites, beaten
2/3 cup instant milk powder
2 Tbsp. raisins
3/4 cup crunchy, non-sugared cereal
1 apple, grated
12 nuts

Mix all ingredients together. Spread into a Pam-sprayed 8" square pan. Bake at 350° until brown.

PIES: *BAKED PIES*
Pumpkin Cheese Pie

1 cup canned pumpkin
1 12-oz. carton cottage cheese
2 eggs
1 slice bread
1/4 cup brown sugar sweetener
1 tsp. pumpkin pie spice

Using blender, mix all ingredients until very smooth. Pour into skinny pie crust and bake at 325° for 40 minutes. To reduce the calories, bake without crust in pan sprayed with vegetable oil. Serves 6-8.

Pumpkin Pie

Filling:
2 cups canned pumpkin
1 cup skim milk
pinch of salt
2 Tbsp. liquid sweetener
1/2 tsp. cinnamon
1/2 tsp. ginger
1/4 tsp. nutmeg
1/4 tsp. cloves

Combine filling ingredients. Pour into shallow dish and bake at 325° until browned. Top with *Whipped Topping.*

Whipped Topping:
3 Tbsp. water
1/2 tsp. unflavored gelatin
1 Tbsp. sweetener
1/3 cup instant milk powder

Mix water, gelatin, sweetener, and milk powder together; chill for 3 hours. Beat until topping stands in peaks. May add vanilla or cinnamon.

Blueberry-Apple Pie

2 medium apples
2 cups fresh *or* frozen blueberries
3 envelopes unflavored gelatin
2 cups diet grape soda
2 drops butter flavoring
2 tsp. liquid sweetener
1 tsp. vanilla
2 tsp. cinnamon
1/8 cup lemon juice
2/3 cup instant milk powder

Reserving 1/2 cup grape soda, place first 8 ingredients in saucepan. Simmer until blueberries and apples are soft. Meanwhile, put gelatin and 1/2 cup soda in small pan and heat until gelatin dissolves. Add to blueberry-apple mixture. Let set slightly. Pour into a non-stick, 8" square cake pan. Sprinkle top with milk powder. Bake at 325° about 5 minutes or until top is golden brown. Chill.

Squash Pie

2 10-oz. pkgs. frozen summer squash
1/4 cup cold water
2 envelopes unflavored gelatin
1/4 cup boiling water
1/2 tsp. pumpkin pie spice
1/3 cup instant milk powder
3/4 tsp. vanilla
sweetener to taste

Cook squash according to package directions. Pour cold water into blender and sprinkle gelatin over it to soften. Add hot water and blend. Add squash and remaining ingredients; blend until smooth. Pour into foil pie pan; place in larger pan containing 1/2" hot water. Bake at 350° for 30 minutes or until firm. Cool and add *Whipped Topping.*

Whipped Topping:
1/2 cup chilled skim milk
1/4 tsp. vanilla
1/4 tsp. lemon juice
sweetener to taste

Combine all ingredients in chilled

mixing bowl. Whip until stiff peaks are formed. Serve at once.

Three-In-One Fruit Pie

1 cup pineapple juice
sweetener to equal 1/2 cup sugar
1 tsp. vanilla
1 large apple, pared, cored, and thinly sliced
2 cups frozen or fresh peaches
1 cup crushed pineapple, well drained
1 1/3 cups instant milk powder
sweetener to taste
1 tsp. cinnamon
1 tsp. orange peel
2 envelopes unflavored gelatin
1/2 cup cold water
1/4 cup boiling water

Simmer pineapple juice, sweetener, and vanilla 5 minutes. Pour over fruit mixture. Mix skim milk, sweetener, cinnamon, orange peel, gelatin, and cold water together; then add boiling water to dissolve gelatin. Top fruit with gelatin mixture and bake at 350° in non-stick pan for 20 minutes or until well browned. Cool. Refrigerate 1 hour before serving.

Variation: Use orange juice instead of pineapple.

Sue Wefel

PIES: *ICEBOX PIES*

Strawberry Banana Chiffon Pie

juice of 1 lemon
1 banana, mashed
1 envelope dietetic strawberry gelatin
1 cup boiling water
1 cup buttermilk
1 cup strawberries, fresh or frozen

Pour lemon juice over mashed banana; set aside. Dissolve gelatin in boiling water. Chill until slightly set. Put gelatin, bananas, buttermilk, and strawberries into blender and beat. Pour into a 9" pie pan. Cover with plastic wrap so that no crust forms. Chill until firm.

Variation: Use a crumb crust.

Strawberry Chiffon Pie

Crust:
2 egg whites
dash of salt
sweetener to equal 3 tsp. sugar
1/3 cup instant milk powder

Filling:
1 envelope dietetic strawberry gelatin
1 1/2 cups sugar-free strawberry soda
1/3 cup instant milk powder
1 cup strawberries
sweetener to equal 1/4 cup sugar

For *Crust,* beat egg whites until stiff. Gradually add salt, sweetener, and milk powder. Beat until stiff. Spread mixture evenly into a non-stick 9" pie pan. Bake at 250° about 30 minutes. Meanwhile, make *filling.* Dissolve gelatin in 1/2 cup boiling soda. Add remaining soda, milk powder, berries, and sweetener. Chill. Pour into pie shell and chill again until mixture is set.

Strawberry Pie

12 oz. sugar-free red soda
1 envelope unflavored gelatin
1 Tbsp. lemon juice
1 tsp. strawberry extract
1 envelope dietetic strawberry
  gelatin
4 cups strawberries

Combine first 4 ingredients; cook until gelatin dissolves. Mixture may thicken slightly. Add strawberry gelatin and cool. Add strawberries and pour into pie shells. Serve with dollops of *Whipped Topping*. Makes 2 pies or approximately 12 tarts.

Whipped Topping:
1 1/3 cups instant milk powder
1 envelope unflavored gelatin
1 cup boiling water
1 Tbsp. lemon juice
1 Tbsp. vanilla
1 Tbsp. liquid sweetener

Place milk powder and gelatin in large mixing bowl; dissolve with boiling water. Beat at medium speed. Add lemon juice, vanilla, and sweetener. Beat at high speed about 10 minutes until very, very stiff.

Note: Topping will not settle in refrigerator.

Pat Mattox

Chocolate Pie

Filling:
1 1/2 envelopes unflavored gelatin
3/4 cup boiling water
2 tsp. chocolate extract
2/3 cup instant milk powder
1 tsp. vanilla

brown food coloring
sweetener to taste
Crust:
2 slices bread, crumbed
dash of nutmeg
liquid sweetener to taste

Dissolve gelatin in boiling water. Add remaining ingredients and refrigerate for 1 hour. Mix crust ingredients together and spread into bottom of pie tin. Add filling.

Pineapple Cream Pie #1

1/2 cup evaporated skim milk
1 cup crushed pineapple
1 envelope dietetic lemon gelatin
sweetener to taste
1 Tbsp. lemon juice

Chill evaporated milk in freezer until ice crystals form around edges. Heat pineapple and add gelatin. Stir and refrigerate until syrupy. Beat chilled evaporated milk until thick. Add sweetener and lemon juice; continue to beat until stiff peaks form. Add syrupy pineapple mixture, beating at low speed until light and fluffy. Spoon into an 8" pie plate. Refrigerate until completely set.

Pineapple Cream Pie #2

1 cup crushed pineapple, drained
1/2 cup reserved pineapple juice
1 envelope unflavored gelatin
2/3 cup instant milk powder
sweetener to taste
1/2 tsp. vanilla
1/2 tsp. pineapple extract

Dissolve gelatin in 1/4 cup juice. Boil remaining 1/4 cup juice and add to gelatin. Add milk powder, beating for 8-10 minutes. Add sweetener, vanilla, and pineapple extract. Fold in crushed pineapple. Put in pie pan and set.

Variation: For *Strawberry Pie*, use 1 cup berries and low-cal strawberry soda for liquid. Substitute strawberry extract.

PIES: *PIE SHELLS*

Meringue Shells

3 egg whites, at room temperature
1/8 tsp. salt
1/2 tsp. cream of tartar
liquid sweetener to taste
1/2 tsp. vanilla

Place egg whites in large mixing bowl. Add salt and cream of tartar; beat with electric mixer at high speed until soft peaks form. Add sweetener, beating well on low speed. Add vanilla, and beat for 10 minutes at medium speed until mixture is very stiff and glossy. Cover baking sheet with foil. Drop egg whites by tablespoonfuls onto foil; make an indentation in center of each mound. Bake at 300° for 45 minutes or until shells are dry on outside. Cool and store in sealed container. Fill shells as desired.

Skinny Pie Shell

1/2 cup sifted flour
1/3 tsp. salt
1/4 tsp. baking powder
1/4 cup diet margarine, very soft

Sift flour, salt, and baking powder together in deep bowl. Add margarine; cut in with fork or pastry blender; continue mixing until no pastry sticks to side of bowl. Shape into a ball. Chill one hour or more. Roll out thin and place in a pie tin.

CANDIES

Coconut Mounds

1 12-oz. can sugar-free creme soda
3 tsp. cocoa
2 tsp. coconut extract
sweetener to taste
1/3 cup instant milk powder
4 envelopes unflavored gelatin

Dissolve gelatin in 6 oz. heated soda. Add remaining ingredients; blend well. Pour into an 8" square pan and set.

Butterscotch Fudge Balls

1-qt. pkg. low-cal chocolate milk powder
1 cup dry oats
4 Tbsp. crunchy peanut butter
1 cup chopped bean sprouts, washed
1 tsp. vanilla
1 tsp. butternut flavoring
1/2 can water chestnuts, chopped
5 Tbsp. sweetener, *optional*

Mix all ingredients together. Roll into small balls. Freeze and eat.

Licorice Drops

5 envelopes unflavored gelatin
3-4 cups boiling water
2-3 tsp. dietetic lime or cherry
   gelatin
sweetener to taste
anise or peppermint extract to taste
red or green food coloring

Add boiling water to gelatin and stir.
Cool; add extract and food coloring.
Pour into an 8" square pan. Chill.
Cut into squares.

Marshmallows

4 envelopes unflavored gelatin
1 cup sugar-free creme soda
1 cup instant milk powder
1/2 tsp. vanilla
2 drops butter flavoring
1 tsp. orange extract
16 pkgs. granulated sweetener

Stir gelatin into soda; add milk
powder and beat. Place over low heat
to dissolve gelatin. Add flavorings
and gradually add sweetener. Beat
until thick. Pour into an 8" square
pan and chill. Cut into squares when
cool.

Peanut Butter Cups

Peanut Butter Filling:
1 envelope unflavored gelatin
1/2 cup water
3 Tbsp. creamy peanut butter
Chocolate Filling:
2 envelopes low-cal chocolate milk
   powder

2 envelopes unflavored gelatin
1/4 cup skim milk
1/2 cup water

For *Peanut Butter Filling*, dissolve
gelatin in water. Bring to a boil and
add peanut butter. Stir to dissolve.
Pour 1/2 mixture into a non-stick,
8" square pan; reserve other half,
keeping it heated so it doesn't set.
Mix *Chocolate Filling* ingredients together; heat to dissolve gelatin.
Cool; then pour over peanut butter
mixture. Refrigerate to set. Top with
remaining peanut butter mixture.
Refrigerate. Cut into bars when set.

Variation: Swirl peanut butter mixture through the chocolate *before*
mixtures set.

Sue Wefel

Jo's Favorite Candy

2/3 cup instant milk powder
1 tsp. sweetener
1 tsp. almond extract
6 tsp. cold water

Combine all ingredients and drop
by teaspoonfuls onto waxed paper.
Eat right away.

Variation: Use other flavorings such
as banana, pineapple, or chocolate.

Note: This is about as calorie free a
candy recipe as you'll find anywhere!
Do count the milk as part of your
milk portion, but forget about
counting the other ingredients.

Chocolate-Covered Raisins

1 tsp. granulated sugar substitute
1/3 cup instant milk powder
1 tsp. cocoa
2 Tbsp. orange juice
1 tsp. vanilla
2 Tbsp. raisins

Combine all ingredients. Drop by 1/2 teaspoonfuls onto waxed paper. Freeze and eat.

Note: These are so good that you'd better make only one batch at a time.

Turkish Delight

6 pkgs. unflavored gelatin
3 cups cold water
1/4 tsp. salt
6 Tbsp. liquid sweetener
6 oz. frozen, unsweetened juice concentrate *or* flavorings of your choice

Soften gelatin a few minutes in cold water. Then heat to dissolve gelatin. Add juice or flavorings, blending well. Pour mixture into Pam-sprayed pans and chill until firm. Cut into squares before serving.

Variations: Use 6 oz. unsweetened fruit juice in place of the juice concentrate. Add more sweetener, if desired.

Note: Remember to count fruit juices in your daily menu planning. Flavorings are unlimited!

Hot & Cold Beverages

When you find yourself craving food out of boredom, anxiety, exhaustion, or restlessness, try a revitalizing beverage. Sip it slowly, savoring the physical and spiritual refreshment which comes from simple things. Then, recall the words of the Lord:

But the water I give . . . becomes a perpetual spring within them. . . .

John 4.14 (TLB)

POINTERS TO HEALTHFUL EATING

Fruits and vegetables can be turned into delicious beverages. Also satisfying are milk and sugar-free drinks.

Milk: The need for milk varies according to age, yet even adults need the calcium, phosphorus, and protein found in 2 servings of milk. Children up to five years of age do well on whole milk; thereafter, reconstituted non-fat instant milk is fine. Four servings or more daily fill the average child's milk requirements.

Fruit Juices: One-half cup juice equals one portion of fruit. For children, a mixture of 1/2 cup fruit juice and 1/2 cup club soda or sugar-free soda makes a very good substitute for sugar-laden drinks.

Tomato Juice: Eight ounces per day is a nice bonus to your regular intake of fruits and vegetables. In fact, other vegetable juices (carrot, especially) make excellent additions to your daily vegetable intake!

HOT

Buttered Rum Coffee

4 cups boiling water
12 tsp. instant coffee
2 tsp. rum extract
8 whole cloves
1/2 tsp. butter flavoring
6 drops sweetener
1/2 cup evaporated skim milk

To boiling water, add all ingredients, reserving cinnamon sticks for garnish. Makes 4 cups.

Hot Toddy Tea

1 tsp. orange peel
dash of cinnamon
2 whole cloves
1 tea bag
2 cups boiling water
4 drops sweetener

Combine all ingredients except sweetener; steep 5 minutes. Sweeten to taste. Serve hot.

Hot Tomato Bouillon

2 cups boiling water
2 beef bouillon cubes
12 oz. tomato juice
1 tsp. Worchestershire sauce
dash of ground pepper
thin lemon slices

In saucepan, combine all ingredients, except pepper and lemon. Bring to boiling point. Serve in mugs with ground pepper and lemon slice on each.

Hot Tomato Cocktail

1 large can tomato juice
3 cups water
3 beef bouillon cubes
1 tsp. onion flakes
1 tsp. horseradish
1 tsp. Worcestershire sauce

Combine all ingredients in saucepan. Heat just to boiling. Serve immediately. Serves 8.

Spiced Holiday Punch

2 qts. water
2 cinnamon sticks
1/2 tsp. ginger
2 whole cloves
sweetener to taste
2 cups apple juice
2 cups strong tea
2 cups orange juice
1/3 cup lemon juice
lemon slices

Combine water, spices, and enough sweetener to make a very sweet syrup. Bring to a boil and boil 15 minutes. Cool, cover, and refrigerate overnight. Strain; combine with juices and tea. Heat. Garnish with lemon slices and serve.

Spiced Tea Nectar

2 cups water
3 Constant Comment tea bags
1 18-oz. can unsweetened apricot
   juice
1 tsp. lemon juice
4 drops sweetener

Boil water in saucepan. Add tea bags and steep 5 minutes. Remove tea bags. Add juices and sweetener. Heat and serve.

COLD: FRUIT-FLAVORED

Banana-Orange Shake

1 6-oz. carton low-fat plain yogurt
1/2 cup orange juice
1/2 banana, sliced
sweetener, optional

Place all ingredients in blender; cover and blend on medium speed 15-20 seconds until smooth.

Variation: For immediate serving, add 4 ice cubes while blending; otherwise, chill for 1 hour before drinking.

Cantaloupe Cooler

1/2 medium cantaloupe
1 pt. sugar-free orange soda
8 oz. sugar-free cherry soda
dash of cinnamon
mint leaves

Cut rind from cantaloupe and cut into chunks. Toss with 1/2 the orange soda. Add remaining orange soda. Pour cherry soda into pitcher. Add cantaloupe mixture and chill. When serving, garnish with dash of cinnamon and mint. Serves 4.

Cold Duck Special

2 bottles sugar-free black cherry soda
1 can sugar-free lemon-lime soda
1/4 cup wine vinegar

Chill all ingredients. Combine and serve.

Creamy Pineapple Malt

4 oz. sugar-free pineapple soda
1/3 cup instant milk powder
1/2 cup crushed pineapple
6 ice cubes
dash of nutmeg

Place all ingredients, except nutmeg, in blender; process at high speed. Add nutmeg and serve.

Fruit Punch

large bottle low-cal cranberry juice
large bottle sugar-free orange soda
16 oz. sugar-free citrus soda
orange slices
pineapple chunks

Mix all ingredients together and pour over ice. Garnish with orange slices and pineapple chunks on toothpicks.

Grapefruit Cooler

1 oz. grapefruit juice, unsweetened
ice cubes
4 oz. sugar-free citrus soda
lemon wedge

Pour grapefruit juice over ice cubes in glass. Add soda. Serve with lemon wedge in frosty glass.

Hawaiian Punch

3 cups unsweetened pineapple juice
1 1/2 cups unsweetened orange juice
3/4 cup unsweetened lemon juice
2 tsp. sweetener
2 qts. carbonated water, chilled

Combine juices and sweetener. Chill. Add carbonated water just before serving.

Jogger Nog

1 cup pineapple juice
1/2 cup plain yogurt
6 ice cubes

Combine all ingredients in blender. Cover and process on high speed until well blended. Serves 2.
Cheryl Doyle

Lemonade #1

2 cups boiling water
5 tea bags or 5 tsp. tea powder
10 whole cloves
1/4 tsp. cinnamon
1/4 tsp. ginger
3/4 cup fresh or concentrated lemon
  juice
sweetener to taste
2 cups ice water
ice cubes

Pour boiling water over tea, cloves, cinnamon, and ginger. Add lemon juice and steep for 5 minutes. Strain into pitcher; add sweetener, ice water, and ice cubes. Stir briskly.

Lemonade #2

1 cup unsweetened lemon juice
2 qts. cold water
1 Tbsp. liquid sweetener
mint leaves
lemon slices

Combine first 3 ingredients in serving container. Just before serving, add ice cubes. Garnish with mint leaves and lemon slices.

Lemon Frappé

1 small pkg. dietetic lemon gelatin
1/2 cup boiling water
2 Tbsp. lemon or lime juice
2 1/2 cups crushed ice

Place gelatin and boiling water in blender; blend until dissolved. Add lemon juice; blend until light and fluffy. Add crushed ice and blend 3-4 minutes until slightly thick. Serve at once. Makes 3 cups.

Melon Pick-Me-Up

4 ice cubes
1/2 cantaloupe, cut in chunks
1/2 tsp. vanilla
3 Tbsp. instant milk powder

Blend all ingredients in blender until thick and creamy.
Alpha Eckstein

Frosty Orange Julio

4 oz. orange juice
2/3 cup instant milk powder
8 drops sweetener
15 ice cubes

Blend all ingredients, adding ice cubes one at a time through top of blender. Blend until ice is crushed. Serves two.

Piña Colada

1/4 fresh or 1/2 small can pineapple
8 ice cubes
2 oz. instant milk powder
4 oz. water
1 tsp. rum extract
1 1/2 tsp. coconut extract
8 drops sweetener

Blend ingredients together and serve.
Nancy Gates

Pineapple-Orange Punch

1 large can frozen orange-pineapple
   juice
water
sweetener to taste
2 qts. sugar-free ginger ale
lime or orange slices

Mix juice and water as listed on can.
Add sweetener and ginger ale. Chill.
Garnish with fruit slices.

Rum Punch

2 tsp. rum extract
1 tsp. pineapple extract
1 tsp. orange extract
1/2 tsp. lemon extract
1 Tbsp. lime juice
4 ice cubes
club soda
sweetener
dash of nutmeg

Combine extracts, lime juice, and
ice cubes in an 8-oz. glass. Fill with
soda water and stir. Sweeten to taste
and sprinkle with nutmeg. Serve well
chilled.

Strawberry Sensation

1 cup skim milk
1/2 cup frozen strawberries,
   unsweetened
1 tsp. vanilla
sweeten to taste

Put all ingredients in blender and
blend until thick.

Thin-And-Tonic

ice cubes
6 oz. club soda
lime slice
sweetener

Pour club soda over ice cubes in a
glass. Squeeze lime juice into glass.
Add sweetener to taste.

Tropical Punch

2 oz. lime juice
2 oz. water
sweetener to taste
1/2 tsp. rum extract
1/2 tsp. brandy extract
1/4 tsp. almond extract

Mix all ingredients together.

Valentine Punch

12 oz. sugar-free black cherry soda
12 oz. sugar-free strawberry soda
16 oz. club soda
1/3 cup vinegar
orange or lime slices

Combine all ingredients. Serve over
cracked ice. Garnish with fruit slices.

Tropical Sparkle

1/2 cup unsweetened lemon juice
3 cups water
1/2 cup lime juice
green food coloring
1 qt. sugar-free lemon-lime soda

Combine all ingredients, except soda. Add soda before serving to retain carbonation. Yields 2 quarts.

Special Sangria

8 oz. sugar-free grape soda
1/2 tsp. orange extract
1 tsp. brandy extract
ice cubes
1 cinnamon stick
1 orange slice

Combine soda and extracts. Pour over ice cubes in tall glass. Garnish with cinnamon stick and orange slice. Serves 1.

COLD: VEGETABLE-FLAVORED

Tomato Cocktail

6 oz. tomato juice
dash of Worcestershire sauce
dash of pepper
dash of hot sauce, *optional*
lime slices

Combine all ingredients and pour over shaved ice. Garnish with lime slices.

Sauerkraut Juice Cocktail

1 Tbsp. lemon juice
1/8 tsp. caraway seeds
2 ice cubes
4 oz. sauerkraut juice

Combine juice and seeds in glass. Add ice cubes and sauerkraut juice. Stir well.

COLD: MISCELLANEOUS

Mocha Malted

1/3 cup instant milk powder
1 cup boiling water
3/4 tsp. instant coffee
4 drops sweetener
1 tsp. chocolate extract
1/8 tsp. almond extract

Blend all ingredients until well mixed.

Variation: Serve with a spoonful of whipped evaporated skim milk with sweetener added.

St. Paddy's Peppermint Brew

1/3 cup instant milk powder
1/2 cup cold water
1 tsp. vanilla extract
1/4 tsp. peppermint extract
sweetener to equal 2 tsp. sugar
2 drops green food coloring
6-8 ice cubes, crushed

Place all ingredients in blender; process at moderate speed until brew is thick and creamy.

Root Beer Cooler

1 cup sugar-free lemon soda *or*
   ginger ale
1 cup sugar-free root beer
1 tsp. peppermint extract
3-5 ice cubes
fresh mint

Mix all ingredients in blender. Garnish with mint.

Spicy Tea Mix

1 cup instant unsweetened
   tea powder
1 24-oz. pkg. unsweetened lemonade
   soft drink mix
1/4 tsp. ground cinnamon
1/4 tsp. ground cloves
1/3 cup granulated sweetener

Place all ingredients in a 1-qt. screw-top jar. Shake gently to mix. Makes about 1 cup mix.

For *Iced Tea:* Measure 2 rounded tsp. into tall glass; add cold water and ice.

For *Hot Tea:* Measure 1 rounded tsp. into cup; fill with boiling water.

Pink Lady Cocktail

1 cup skim milk
1/8 tsp. rum extract
4 drops sweetener
1 drop red food coloring
3 ice cubes

Combine all ingredients. Serve in tall stemmed cocktail glass. Yields 1 serving.

Low-Cal Instant Chocolate Mix

1 lb. *or* 5 3.2-oz. pkgs. instant milk
   powder
3/4 cup cocoa
10 Tbsp. granulated sweetener

Mix all ingredients well and store in tightly covered jar.

To make 1 cup of hot cocoa: Add 1/3 cup of mix and enough boiling water to fill a cup. Process in blender for a better texture.

To make a cold chocolate shake: Add 1/3 cup of mix, 6 ice cubes, and 1 cup water to blender; process at high speed.

GENERAL NUTRITION GUIDE

Why nutrition is important
Good health for you and your family is a feeling of total well-being, physically, psychologically, and emotionally. Nutrition plays an important part in good health because it affects your skin, teeth, eyes, hair, and overall appearance, as well as your personality, behavior, working potential, and general outlook on life!

Requirements for energy and for nutrients, such as protein, vitamins, and minerals, vary with age, life-style, and level of activity. Within your family, there may be different nutrient needs. For example, during certain stages of growth and reproduction, the need for calcium and vitamin D is greater than at other times; energy requirements are high during the teen years because of growth and development.

Life-style and activity play a major role in determining energy needs. A lumberjack uses up more energy than an office worker. Playing cards takes less exertion than cross-country skiing. If you continue to eat the same amount of food throughout your life, you'll probably gradually gain weight, because the body metabolism slows down and the activity level usually drops as people get older.

Although eating habits, both good and bad, are formed early in life, it's never too late to begin following the path to good nutrition. Canada's Food Guide can help you eat wisely and well.

Canada's Food Guide
Let's begin by emphasizing that Canada's Food Guide is not a rigid set of rules. It's a pattern of eating through which you and your family can obtain the more than 50 nutrients needed by your bodies every day.

The Guide recommends daily numbers of servings to be selected from each of the four food groups:

- Milk and milk products
- Bread and cereals
- Fruits and vegetables
- Meat and alternates

These four food groups were chosen because the kinds and amounts of key nutrients each group supplies form an interlocking pattern of good nutrition, much like a jigsaw puzzle. But, just as pieces of a puzzle are not interchangeable because they are all different, these food groups are not interchangeable because the nutrients in them differ. For example, extra vitamin C from the Fruits and Vegetables group can't make up for the shortage of vitamin D that can occur if the Milk and Milk Products group is neglected.

Each food group contributes a number of specific, essential nutrients, as listed in the table that follows. You wouldn't expect to complete a jigsaw puzzle without having all the pieces. In the same way, good nutrition and complete health are difficult if some of the nutrients are missing.

Main nutrients contributed by the food groups

Nutrient	Major functions	Milk and milk products	Bread and cereals	Fruits and vegetables	Meat and alternates
Carbohydrate	Supplies energy. Assists in the utilization of fats. Spares protein.		●	●	
Fat	Supplies energy. Aids in the absorption of fat soluble vitamins.	●			●
Protein	Builds and repairs body tissues. Builds antibodies to fight infection.	●	●		●
Vitamin A	Aids normal bone and tooth development. Maintains the health of the skin and lining membranes. Permits good night vision.	●		●	●
B Vitamins Thiamin	Releases energy from carbohydrates. Aids normal growth and appetite. Maintains normal function of the nervous system and gastrointestinal tract.		●	●	●
Riboflavin	Maintains healthy skin and eyes. Maintains a normal nervous system. Releases energy to body cells during metabolism.	●	●		●
Niacin	Aids normal growth and development. Maintains normal function of the nervous system and gastrointestinal tract.		●	●	●
Folic acid	Aids red blood cell formation.			●	●
Vitamin C	Maintains healthy teeth and gums. Maintains strong blood vessel walls.			●	
Vitamin D	Enhances calcium and phosphorus utilization in the formation and maintenance of healthy bones and teeth.	●			
Calcium	Aids in the formation and maintenance of strong bones and teeth. Permits healthy nerve function and normal blood clotting.	●			
Iron	An essential part of hemoglobin, the red blood cell constituent that transports oxygen and carbon dioxide.		●	●	●

From: INFORMATION SERVICES, CANADA DEPT. OF AGRICULTURE, OTTAWA
Cat. No.: A53-1651/1978 ISBN-0-662-01438-3

FREEZING TIPS: FRUIT
Each fruit = 1 fruit exchange and approximately 40 calories in amounts given below.

Prepare fruits according to chart. Use sweetener as recommended; even better, use less than suggested! Select good quality fruit; freeze quickly to avoid discoloration. Work with small quantities of fruit at a time. To package the fruit, fill a container about 1/3 full of cold water. Place fruit in container to within 1/2" of top. Add sweetener to fruit. To keep fruit immersed in solution, place a piece of crumpled wax paper over top of fruit. Cover, label, and freeze. Yields about 1 quart.

Type of Fruit	Amount and Preparation	Other Ingredients	Serving Portion
Blueberries	3 pints Wash and clean.	2 cups cold water 9 drops sweetener	2/3 cup
Cantaloupe melon	Allow 1 1/2 cups fruit per pint. Wash, halve, and remove seeds. Cut into balls or cubes.	Same as blueberries	2/3 cup
Cherries	2 to 3 pounds. Wash and pit, if desired.	2 cups cold water 6 drops sweetener 1/4 tsp. ascorbic acid	10 large
Peaches	2 pounds Wash, peel, and slice.	2 cups cold water 9 drops sweetener 1/2 tsp. ascorbic acid	1/2 cup
Pineapple	Allow 1 1/2 cups pineapple per pint. Peel, core, and dice.	Same as blueberries	1/2 cup
Strawberries	6 pints Clean and slice. Toss with solution. Fill containers and freeze.	1/2 cup cold water 6 drops sweetener	2/3 cup

FREEZING TIPS: GENERAL FREEZING

Set freezer temperature control at the coldest point a day before freezing foods. It should be between 10 and 20 degrees below zero. Store frozen foods at 0. Label every package with name of food and freezing date. Practice the rule, "first in, first out." Organize your freezer so that food which has been in longest will be used soonest.

Packaging is important. Use heavy-duty foil, transparent freezer films, freezer paper, or plastic bags to keep out moisture and vapor. When wrapping or packaging food, make as airtight as possible to prevent formation of ice crystals on the food.

FRUIT CANNING TIPS

Each fruit = 1 fruit exchange and approximately 40 calories in amounts given below.

Prepare fruit according to chart. In saucepan, combine fruit and sweetener. Bring to a boil. Pack into sterilized jars, filling to jar shoulder with fruit. Fill to within 1/2" of top with sweetener. Seal jars. Process in boiling water bath for 20 minutes. Cool. Yields 2 pints.

Avoid the "open kettle" method because fruits are fragile and lose more color. The boiling water bath assures a better seal, while fruit retains better shape.

Type of Fruit	Amount and Preparation of Fruit	Other Ingredients	Serving Portion
Apples	2 pounds Peel, core, and slice	2 cups water 3 drops sweetener	3/4 cup
Apricots	2 to 3 pounds Wash, halve, and remove pits	2 cups water 9 drops sweetener 1 Tbsp. lemon juice	4 halves
Cherries	2 to 3 pounds Wash and pit, if desired	Same as apricots	10 large
Peaches	2 to 3 pounds Peel, halve, and remove stone	Same as apricots	2 halves
Pears	2 to 3 pounds Peel, halve, and core	Same as apricots	2 halves
Plums	2 to 2 1/2 pounds Wash and prick skins	Same as apricots	2 whole

INDEX

EXTRA RECIPES

EXTRA RECIPES

EXTRA RECIPES

EXTRA RECIPES